MAKING UP FOR

LOST TIME

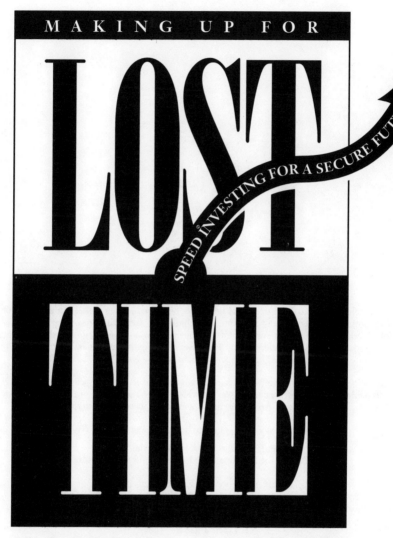

MAKING UP FOR LOST TIME

SPEED INVESTING FOR A SECURE FUTURE

ADRIANE G. BERG

Hearst Books   New York

LIBRARY OF CONGRESS CATALOGING-IN-PUBLICATION DATA

Berg, Adriane G. (Adriane Gilda), 1948–
Making up for lost time: speed investing for a secure future /
          p.   cm.
Includes bibliographical references and index.
ISBN 0-688-11938-7
1. Finance, Personal.   2. Investments.   3. Portfolio management.
I. Title.
HG179.B44   1994
332.024—dc20   93-35448
CIP

Printed in the United States of America

First Edition

1 2 3 4 5 6 7 8 9 10

BOOK DESIGN BY PATRICE FODERO

To all my friends
who can remember dancing to a Johnny Mathis song in a finished basement,
and to my children, Arthur and Rosie,
who never will.

ACKNOWLEDGMENTS

I would like to thank the following experts in the field of investment and money management for their invaluable help and their dedication to helping others make a better future.

Richard T. Adams, Jr., assistant vice president of Merrill Lynch; Bruce Baumgarten, first senior vice president of Gibraltar Securities; Charles Hamowy, CFP, CPA, with IDS Financial Services; Michael Mathias, CFP, chairman of the board of Interstate Financial Group; Robert Paduano, principal, Kirlin Securities, Inc.; Lee Rosenberg, CFP, vice president of ARS Financial Services, Inc.; Harold Seigel, president of FSG International; Steven Selengut, president of Sanco Services, Inc.; and Glenn Toussaint, CFP with Toussaint Financial Associates.

Contents

Personal and Confidential . . .

Before we begin, I would like you to know that my credentials for writing this book are impeccable. Although I am considered one of the nation's leading experts in personal finance, I, myself, must make up for lost time! In the past twenty years, I have been a lightning rod for all the feelings of fear, regret, anger, and (above all) triumph that you too will feel in the process of *making up for lost time*.

By the time I was eleven years old, I understood better than most that even good, hardworking people can end up with very few assets if they fail to plan. That was the year my father at age forty-two died suddenly and without financial preparation.

Since then I have practiced law, become a stockbroker and financial planner, and even served a stint as an insurance salesperson. Throughout, I earned a great deal of money. And in the late eighties, as a real estate developer, I became a multimillionaire. But only on paper. In fact, I would never be qualified to write this success book if two real estate projects had not failed.

The real estate crash of the late eighties not only took my holdings but left me in substantial debt to the creditors of my projects.

From that I learned the futility of regret and self-blame, and the pain of diminishing my family's future. However, I also learned the nobility of taking responsibility. From that time on, I have been amazed at how abundant the world really is; how almost mystically good things happen if you let them. And in the past four years I have explored every aspect of making up for lost time.

I have written several finance books and have lectured around the world on creating and saving wealth. I have gained an intense education in taxes as host of FNN's *IRS Tax Beat*. Constantly studying investment strategy, I've become a walking encyclopedia of investment information. I have given investment advice on my WABC radio show, numerous other television shows, in my newspaper columns, and at my nationwide seminars on wealth building.

Oh yes. And at age forty-three, I also had my second child.

If I have been able to rebuild this way, so can you, in your own special way. Like you, I am an ordinary person who has faced extraordinary circumstances. I have learned that adversity can make you strong. I have mentioned all this so you won't think me an ivory tower–dwelling advice giver who doesn't understand how hard it is to believe in a bright future during a dim present.

This book will help you get your past behind you and move full speed ahead. It contains a substantial amount of hard-core investment advice and distills the most important financial facts to show you how to meet your financial goals faster than you thought possible. I will give you tidbits of information and experience that helped me implement the investment advice I am sharing with you. In these pages you will find everything from detailed tips on saving money on college costs to sophisticated strategies for global investing. Your success will be achieved through implementing a combination of very practical knowledge and a very broad philosophy. So read on and start making up for lost time!

I
t's Never Too Late to Be a Financial Success

WATCH OUR SMOKE! HOW WE WILL TRIUMPH OVER OUR ECONOMIC PAST

My idea of success is personal freedom . . . From everything—
from money, from poverty, from ease and anxiety. To keep a kind
of Republic of the spirit—that's what I call success.

EDITH WHARTON
The House of Mirth

If you have twenty-five years or less until retirement or ten years
or less before your eldest child enters college, you most likely need
to make up for a lot of years during which you didn't save, got into
debt, and relied too heavily on your house as a resource for your
retirement.

You're certainly not alone. Seventy-eight million baby boomers
nationwide, and 1 billion worldwide, are with you. As our financial
clock starts ticking, we begin to shed that "illusion of unlimited
wealth" we fantasized in the eighties and really start to get down
to business.

In this book, you will find

- A three-tier system of investing that builds wealth with speed
  and safety

- A quick way to improve money habits
- An easy budget for us old souls set in our ways
- A review of pension tips that help you retire in style
- A look at investments and programs guaranteed to pay for higher education
- A selection of tax tips to help you keep all the income and profit you can
- A new approach to real estate so you can keep your American Dream
- A "debt detoxification" program to help you get your liabilities behind you
- Help in handling your parents' financial problems

  and

- Advice for selecting and working with financial professionals and institutions so you can cut paperwork, reduce anxiety, and spend less of your precious time on personal money matters

Let's face it, confusion over personal finance comes as no surprise. We never learned it in school, and our parents often didn't teach it to us. We resent every moment we spend on preparing taxes, comparing home mortgage rates, and waiting in line at the bank. We are amazed at the sheer volume of paper we must manage and the records we must keep just to know where we are financially.

As a generation we have lived through more trends and more economic cycles than any other generation in the two hundred years since the birth of the United States. And now, at an age when we have paid our dues and deserve peace of mind, many of us must start from scratch, build new dreams, revise lifelong goals.

And our material expectations are very high. We have developed expensive tastes. As we grow older, we want money for the freedom to travel, to be creative, and to live nicely. We wonder whether we'll ever take that year's sabbatical, write that novel, or buy that farm.

We are surprised at how much of our life's energy goes to pay for our insurance, our child's orthodontist, our mortgage.

And then there are our parents. We are tied to them in new ways. They may be dependent on us, or we on them. No matter which, it is all very unexpected.

It took four years to craft this book, and it was a grand adventure. I lived in a commune, attended corporate meetings at the highest level, listened to top economists and spiritual gurus. I followed the lives of people all over the world to see how different financial lifestyles really work. I tracked investment strategies to see what good they can do us. And I came to one conclusion: *The time we have lost, we can reclaim!*

These are the factors that will take us to the top:

Longevity Thanks to advances in medicine, we can expect to live a very long time. We have an extra ten years of work life, if we need it, to make up for lost time.

Education The same analytic skills, drive, and education that distinguish us as a group will make us a success as individuals.

Maturity We now have the perspective and experience we need to be financial successes.

Mass Communications Don't underestimate the importance of the media in helping us make up for lost time. We can start pizza shops in Poland, bank in other states, find out how orange crops are doing in California, and follow thousands of stock offerings while we drink our coffee in the morning. We are the beneficiaries of unprecedented informational tools.

Necessity The road did not rise up to meet us. We need to make up for lost time to make our long future a healthy and happy one.

Yet, with all these going for us, we still need a lot of know-how, which this book can provide.

How to Make the Best Use of This Book

If you don't know where you are going, any road will take you there.

LEWIS CARROLL
Alice's Adventures in Wonderland

To get the most out of this book, first read it through once to get the big picture of what you want to achieve. Discuss it or even read it together with your co-decision maker.

Then as you go about your personal financial business (i.e., paying bills, contributing to your pension, and so on), be on the alert for the information you need to answer the personal money and goal questions asked in the book. Gather the credit card statements, bills, financial documents, and anything else you'll need to complete the investment and budget exercises you'll find in the book.

Go get some pencils. Clear a comfortable space. Have paper, a pencil sharpener, a calculator (or ten toes and fingers) at the ready. Use a spreadsheet if you like, or yellow paper if that's your style. It all works, but only if you do.

Then do another read with pencil and paper in hand. Pay special attention to the charts, graphs, and formulas when you get to them; they are designed to give you quick help in making up for lost time. If, like me, you have a tendency to skip "the math part," don't! Use a calculator or get help, but work with the numbers. Information is as much a tool of financial planning as money is. You can't make up for lost time without some calculation. There are "as painless as possible forms" to note everything from net worth to how many stocks you bought on tips from your brother-in-law. There are formulas—most of which you should have been taught in high school—that show you how interest compounds, and whether you need tax-free or taxable investments, and more.

You will also find a number of Silent Surveys, or questionnaires, designed to explore your financial past and present, inner feelings, and hang-ups about money and success. Their purpose is to convert hopes and dreams into goals, fears and troubles into creative challenge. Don't gloss over them. Answer the questions in a dialogue with yourself. Take them without the influence of your partner and let your partner take them without your interference. Write what is true for you. If you feel like writing more, do so. It means that a particular question is important to you.

When you have made your investment and other financial choices, before you take action, supplement the knowledge you have learned from the text with the material from the Bibliography. Most of us have learned about money and investments in the school of hard knocks. The purpose of this book is to give you a smoother ride, with each part offering you the technical basics and comprehensive knowledge you will need to carry out the strategies and ideas that help make up for lost time.

Above all, take action. To make up for lost time, you are about to

- Change negative money habits
- Determine your net worth
- Set goals for success
- Pick investments that meet your goals in the time you have
- Make those investments
- Implement new and economical strategies that meet big needs like housing and college
- Perhaps relocate and/or change careers

That's how you make up for lost time. If it seems impossible, remember this: *The magic is in the doing!*

ONE LAST LOOK BACK

(WITHOUT TURNING INTO SALT)

No moment is ever lost in time, it is always there.

KURT VONNEGUT,
interview in *In Flight* magazine

In the years from our college and high school graduations until the present, our nation went into an economic tailspin from which it has never recovered. Since 1954 there have been no fewer than eight recessions. Yet, as children of the Eisenhower years we got our earliest impressions of money in a stable and calm economy. None of us dreamed that forty years later we would expend so much time and energy on money: making it, spending it, or worrying about it. Many of us wonder what we did wrong to be in a financial fix after forty, or at best, to be so far below our financial expectations. Nothing in our upbringing could have prepared us for the twenty years of economic turmoil that began when we were young adults and have lasted to the present.

In one way or another, most of us tend to regard our financial past with regret, blame, or shame. We often procrastinate in making financial decisions because we don't trust our own judgment. This reaction is only natural. Let's take one last look backward to see why we are not to blame.

As Young Adults, We Were Singularly Unprepared to Deal with Finances

Woodstock 1969 has become a metaphor for our youth. A powerful thing happened to hundreds of thousands of us now between the ages of forty and sixty. Many of us harbored a deep conviction that money was a danger to values, that anything valuable could be had without money. As for Woodstock, it was living proof. For us the sky was the limit. Many of us traveled abroad. We fought for our rights and the rights of others. We rejected compromise.

The need to conform to the workplace came as an emotional shock. Yet financially, life was uncommonly good. Directly after Kennedy's election in 1960 the economy was strong. Jobs were plentiful, unemployment declined, productivity grew, and inflation was just under 2 percent. By 1965, deficit spending as a result of the Vietnam War added a false boom to the economy.

By the time we graduated from college, trade school, or professional school we were earning unheard-of entry-level salaries. Yet many of us refused to bow to material values. We could not foresee how times would change. We certainly did not select our careers based on pensions or fringe benefits.

Our Early Work Years Were Inflationary Years; We Learned to Spend

By the seventies, still young adults, we got the first shock of major economic change: inflation. A rise in oil and food prices led to an unprecedented surge in the cost of cars, electronics, houses, and consumer goods. We thought the spiral would go on forever. We also found ourselves ready to acquire. We were not kids anymore: We needed to furnish apartments, dress for success, and have transportation.

Most of us spent our inflated salaries on inflated-priced goods. We used credit cards to buy today what we anticipated would be more expensive tomorrow. It was the beginning of the debtor economy: Buy now, pay later. Now it's later, and most of us are still paying.

We Did Not Feel Compelled to Save Because We Were Living in Our Bank

The real estate boom of the eighties might have saved us. But once again, we did not anticipate the recession that followed. Most of us did not cash-out fast enough to make the killing on our own houses and other real estate that would have been the substitute for diligent pension planning and disciplined savings. Those who expected to retire on the equity in their house are prime candidates for making up for lost time.

Now, in the nineties, we are ready for a financial plan that will last for a while. We want to be able to send our kids to college, revamp our careers, and build rapidly for the retirement that is approaching. To do this, we must trust ourselves to make decisions. Remember this: *We are the product of our extraordinary economic history. And none of our moments has been lost in time.*

Acknowledge your past, but put it behind you. From now on, don't react to the economy after it has changed. Instead, act before it's too late. In doing this—even if you consider yourself to be "finance-o-phobic"—you will enhance your ability to make up for lost time.

CHAPTER 3

Eight Essential Money Habits That Will Help You Make Up for Lost Time—and How to Acquire Them Quickly

We all lead two lives, the life we learn with and the life we live with after we learn.

GLENN CLOSE
in *The Natural*

Most of us over forty have been handling our own money for a minimum of fifteen years. For those over fifty, it may be closer to thirty years. During this period we have developed some powerful money habits. There are eight habits that relate to money management and investing that must be cultivated immediately in order to make up for lost time. They are very simple to state, but like a diet, they are not so easy to put into practice.

To help you develop or improve any of the habits in which you may be weak, I have provided lists of statements so you can see which apply to you. These are your first Silent Surveys. Each question group ends with your plan of action to implement and encourage each new habit.

No matter how sophisticated you get as an investor, you will never make up for lost time if these eight habits are not practiced. Accordingly, even if you are not a great expert in finance, you will do well if your eight habits are strong.

ESSENTIAL MONEY HABIT 1: KEEP RECORDS

Record keeping can be as important as money. Sometimes record keeping *is* money; that is, if you can't prove a tax deduction, you may not be able to take it. You must acknowledge your money and be in touch with the amount you earn, spend, and save.

Make a place for money in your life. Give it a home: a drawer, a file. The more you keep track of your money, the more money you will get.

SILENT SURVEY

1. I am disciplined when it comes to money matters, including record keeping.
2. I need improvement in
   Checkbook balancing
   Reviewing monthly statements
   Knowing my net worth
   Keeping tax records
   Other
3. My money tasks are pretty fairly divided between and done efficiently by my mate and me; or if I do all the work myself, I do it efficiently.
4. My money procedures, like filing income taxes or making deposits or paying bills, are a monument to negligence.
5. My record-keeping habits aren't terrible, but they need improvement.

Here is my plan: I will create a "boardroom" in my house, and I will set aside one hour every week to work on bookkeeping. I will use a computer program or hire a college student or high school senior looking for part-time work to do the routine tasks like checking the math on my bank statements and recording the number of shares added to my mutual fund(s). I will talk seriously with my mate about sharing the tasks. (Choose all or some of the above.)

ESSENTIAL MONEY HABIT 2: SAVE MONEY

Saving money on a regular basis is a crucial habit. We all could save at least 10 percent of the amount we earn and not feel deprived. This is true even of those of us who feel there is never anything left at the end of the week. By saving money before we spend, we're sure to have something for our future.

SILENT SURVEY

1. I save _____ percent from each paycheck or other source(s) of income.
2. There is never enough money. I save nothing.
3. I save erratically.
4. I am too much in debt to save.

Here is my plan: I will save a minimum of 10 percent from each source of income. Until I have created a full financial plan, I will deposit the amount in a savings account, a money market fund, or a mutual fund just to cultivate the saving habit. I will start this week.

ESSENTIAL MONEY HABIT 3: BE SELECTIVE IN TAKING FINANCIAL ADVICE

It would be lovely to have a financial guru telling us what to do. This natural desire to want others to take financial responsibility leads to major mistakes when we indulge it. Use professionals wisely, but always remain in charge of your own finances.

SILENT SURVEY

1. I rely on the following people to help me make money decisions:

   Spouse

   Accountant

   Lawyer

   Broker

   Financial planner

   Banker

   Money manager

   Parent

   Friend

   Boss

   No one

2. I am satisfied with the consultants I rely on.

3. I am not satisfied with them.

4. I control the financial decisions.

5. They make the final decisions.

6. I am intimidated by my advisers.

7. I am comfortable with them.

Here is my plan: I will read carefully the details on various professional services as profiled in Chapter 15. I will choose the best ones for me. I acknowledge that the decision about bucks stops with me. I acknowledge my power over my own money and my responsibility for it.

ESSENTIAL MONEY HABIT 4: DON'T WORRY ABOUT MONEY; IT INHIBITS CLEAR THINKING

If you feel anxious about money, you will avoid gaining knowledge and taking action. Worrying is not proactive. It can stymie you from making financial progress. It is also habit-forming and self-perpetuating. Worries can grow even when trouble doesn't. Although you will know how to make up for lost time after reading this book, you can worry yourself into inaction.

SILENT SURVEY

1. I worry about money
   In the morning
   At bill time
   At tax time
   At tuition time
   At shopping time
   At investment time
   All the time
   Very little
2. When I worry about money, my worry is about
   Debt
   Job
   House
   Tuition
   Future time
   Past mistakes
   Health care
   Other

Here is my plan: For one week I will give myself a vacation from money worry. I will read this book and implement its advice. Pretty soon

I will get relief from worry because I am actually taking steps to make up for lost time.

ESSENTIAL MONEY HABIT 5: DON'T USE THE PAST AS A POWER SOURCE FOR FAILURE

If you are interested in making up for lost time, then on some level you regret some event, strategy, investment, or deed that took place in the past. Let yourself off the hook. Don't let past mistakes dampen your belief in your ability to make good future decisions. Review the good and bad things you did in the past with respect to money. Repeat the good things. Let the bad ones go.

SILENT SURVEY

1. The best thing I ever did with my money after I was twenty-one years old was
2. I did it because
3. The probability that I can do it again is
4. If I can, I will, by _____ (date)
5. The worst thing I ever did with my money after I was twenty-one was
6. I did it because
7. The warning signs of doing it again are

Here is my plan: I will write out a plan of action to invest in a certain type of stock, do research to see if I can duplicate a past success, think rationally and without blame about the reason for a past mistake, and take steps to guard against its repetition in the future. (Choose the items that best apply to you.)

ESSENTIAL MONEY HABIT 6: DWELL ON YOUR STRENGTHS, NOT YOUR WEAKNESSES

The old adage "the rich get richer" is true. Yet you would be surprised at how often we do not try to repeat our successes. The quickest way to make up for lost time is to let go of your past mistakes and expand on your successes.

SILENT SURVEY

1. My money strengths are
   Earning money through work
   Investing
   Protecting my assets
   Saving
   Acquiring valuable things at good prices
   Managing debt
   Budgeting
   Other
2. My money weaknesses are
   Ignorance of finance
   Greed
   Fear of any risk
   Inflexibility once a decision is made
   Difficulty in taking profits
   Difficulty in selling and taking a loss
   Unwillingness to compromise unrealistic goals
   Undue risk taking
   Undue conservatism

Here is my plan: I will pay careful attention to the calculations I find throughout this book. Every time I draw a conclusion about an action I must take in order to make up for lost time, I will review this list of traits honestly. If I think that I may interfere with the best choice for me, I will work to overcome the problem.

ESSENTIAL MONEY HABIT 7: KNOW YOUR GOAL

Realistic, achievable, and rewarding goals are much easier to articulate after age forty than before. This is the consolation of our age group. We now know what we want. Let's state it and go for it!

SILENT SURVEY

1. My financial goals are (list them in order of priority; eliminate those that do not apply)

   Saving for retirement

   Paying for college

   Being able to travel

   Finding better housing

   Buying a car

   Having consumer goods

   Getting out of debt

   Moving

   Finding a new job

   Generating more income

   Better investing

   Other

2. To meet my financial goals, I would rather (take time with this and consult your mate)

   Make a great financial sacrifice over a short period of time

   Make small financial sacrifices over a long period of time

   Change my goal(s)

Limit the number of goals I have

Work longer hours or get an additional job

Here is my plan: First I will divide my money goals into long- and short-term. Next I will divide my goals into permanent (housing, retirement) and consumable (clothing, car, vacation). Then I will prioritize and continually refine my goals until I have a clear plan for reaching them.

ESSENTIAL MONEY HABIT 8: MAKE DECISIONS DESPITE THE OVERABUNDANT INVESTMENT CHOICES

As of this writing there are 4,300 mutual funds and 2,700 insurance companies to choose from. You can go global, use banks or credit unions, or read financial newsletters ad infinitum. By contrast, our parents had a choice between a toaster and luggage when they decided to open a simple savings account. That was about the extent of investment options for middle-class Americans in their generation. Although the smorgasbord we have can easily freeze us into inactivity, inaction does not make up for lost time.

For this habit of decision making among the great number of available investment choices, I do not have a Silent Survey. Instead, I have a little story called the "Blue Suit Theory of Investing." My media listeners tell me that it helps them overcome the "finance-o-phobia" that comes with the overabundance of choice. It is appropriate to end this chapter on money habits with this little story, not just because it helps you make decisions, but also because it expresses the notion that you need not be perfect in your investment judgment to make up for lost time.

THE BLUE SUIT THEORY OF INVESTING

A man walks into a clothing store to buy a blue suit for work. He finds many different types on the rack. He asks his wife and the salesman for their opinions, and they both choose different suits. The man can't decide which suit he wants. He closes his eyes and buys the first suit he touches. The next day he goes to work wearing his randomly selected blue suit. What goes wrong?

Answer: Nothing. He is wearing a perfectly good suit, appropriate for his setting. It doesn't matter much if the pants have cuffs or not or if the lapel is a little wide or narrow. If he had showed up in a red dress, he'd be in trouble. And if he never bought any clothes at all, he could never even go to work.

Investment choice is like that. Ninety percent of making the right selection is just knowing that you need a blue suit rather than a red dress. If you can fine-tune your choice to get the other 10 percent right, so much the better. That's called "market timing." It's nice, but it's not critical. Eventually, as you buy more suits (investments) your fashion (investment) sense will fine-tune itself. And even if it doesn't, it won't matter much.

CHAPTER 4

A Net Worth Sketch That Doesn't Undermine Your Self-worth

What can it profit a man to gain the whole world and to come to his property with a gastric ulcer, a blown prostate, and bifocals?

JOHN STEINBECK
Cannery Row

It's my job right now to get you over your resistance to quantifying your assets and liabilities, which comes from mixing up your net worth and self-worth. And do we ever do that! Money has a huge place in our self-esteem. It buys prestige in the marketplace, power in politics, and sex in the bedroom. It can elicit approval from parents and admiration from peers.

Many a professional and executive have serious trouble filling out a net worth statement. But people who own their own businesses have it worst of all. They often confuse personal success with the dollar value of their business. Putting net worth on paper is also a stumbling block for couples whose financial secrets are part of their troubled relationship.

It is because we have so much emotion invested in our net worth that we procrastinate in making a tally. But, no matter how you feel about it, you still have to do your net worth statement. Here's why.

- You have to start with the money you already have in order to make up for lost time.
- If you think you have no assets, you could be wrong.
- If you are a millionaire on paper, you may be in danger because of lack of diversification (i.e., all the worth in one piece of property).
- If you have a negative net worth, you may need debt consolidation, a payout plan out with creditors, or to declare bankruptcy in order to get started on making up for lost time.

Doing a net worth statement also will help you

- Know your tax bracket
- Know the amount of life and household insurance you need
- Cultivate the record-keeping habit so you can keep track of how well you are doing in making up for lost time

You can expect that if you follow the making-up-for-lost-time program, your net worth will look much improved six months from now!

So, how are you going to do your net worth statement in the most painless fashion?

First, list and add up your assets. Don't list liabilities and subtract the one from the other. Your total net worth is not important at this stage. Five years ago I knew both millionaires and bankrupts. I still know them today, except that most of them have reversed roles. The bottom line is not important when you get started.

Second, be realistic about the amount of time this should take. Chances are, it will take you a week of checking the value of mutual funds, calling your bank to find out what your money market is paying, and checking with your insurance agent on the cash value of your policy if you have one.

Third, use your net worth statement to organize the investments you already have into three types, which I call the Three Tiers and describe later on in this chapter. This Three-Tier system is the backbone of investing to make up for lost time. By the time you finish this book, your net worth statement will be not merely a record of what you have, but also a chart of which assets should be retained, sold, added to, or changed in some other way.

Fourth, take a Silent Survey on each entry to see how you acquired it. As you think about the history of each acquisition, relate it to the Silent Survey in Chapter 3 regarding advisers and how you make decisions (page 28). In this way you will learn not only which investments are working for you, but who has helped you and whom you should avoid in the future. To make up for lost time, it is important that you get "unstuck" from bad past associations.

SILENT SURVEY

The reason I am not going to actually pick up a pencil and paper and do the net worth statement no matter what you say is

It takes too much time

I own so little that I carry my financial picture around in my head

I own mostly art and antiques and I need appraisals

I can't face my debts

It's my husband's job

It's my wife's job

It's my broker's job

It's a big job and I'm too busy earning money

I'm okay financially, so it's a waste of time

I did it last year

My records are in a mess; as soon as I get them straightened out, I'll do it

Now that you've confronted all your excuses, I'm pleased to present . . .

THE "HOLD YOUR NOSE AND DO IT" NET WORTH STATEMENT

At the end of this chapter you will find a form that I designed for myself when I began my road to making up for lost time. By all means, create your own form if you wish. Just sit down with a pad and pencil, your files, and the telephone. Have a calculator handy. A cooperative mate would be a good idea too—never refuse a helping hand.

Now, compartmentalize your assets into the three tiers outlined below. You will be referring to this compartmentalization several times. You might want to make your list on a handy piece of paper that you use as a bookmark.

TIER-ONE INVESTMENTS

There are two types of Tier-One investments. Tier One A comprises assets that are really cash equivalents, not really investments. I call them ladies-in-waiting; they're waiting for you to turn them into investments. Tier-One-A investments include

Cash on hand
Checking accounts
Money markets
Savings accounts
Cash value of insurance policies

Tier One B comprises those investments from which you derive interest income. They generally have exact maturity dates and some form of guarantee of principal and interest. Technically, you are lending your money to institutions like banks, corporations, and governments in return for interest on your loan. Tier-One-B investments include

Bonds (municipal, corporate, and United States)
Fixed annuities

Income mutual funds that invest in bonds and other income-
producing assets

Zero-coupon bonds, zero-coupon Treasury notes, bills, and
bonds

Mortgages you hold as creditor

Treasuries

Notes

Other investments that produce income, including stocks bought
primarily for dividends (e.g., utilities, as opposed to non-
dividend-paying emerging growth stocks)

Stop here.

These Tier-One-A and Tier-One-B investments are very easy
to tabulate. Your own records, your banker, broker, and mutual
funds' 800 numbers will give you their present value. Where it's
applicable, also jot down the price you paid for them. This gives
you a notion of whether the investment has grown in value. For
interest-bearing investments, write down the interest you are getting and whether it is fixed or variable. Where applicable, note
whether they're inside or outside pension and other tax-deferred
plans and whether they're tax-deferred, taxable, or tax-free.

TIER-TWO INVESTMENTS

Now it's time to list Tier-Two investments. These are ownership
investments, like common and preferred stocks and some real estate,
which have fewer guarantees associated with them. Tier-Two investments include

Stocks bought for growth and income—common stocks and
blue-chip stocks (steady, proven, and good dividend payers)

Stocks bought for growth potential, sometimes called small caps
or mid caps

Business interests

Variable annuities

Stock mutual funds—mid cap, small cap, and aggressive growth funds

Stock options

Royalties, patents, copyrights

Real estate investment trusts (REITs)

Other investment real estate

Other growth investments

To evaluate stocks, all you need is a financial newspaper, your mutual funds' 800 numbers, and the number of your broker. Jot down each stock's acquisition price and its present value. The value of real estate may need an appraisal or at least a broker's opinion. On royalty-generating assets, take your best guess, based on the contract under which you obtained the rights.

For all Tier-Two assets, state whether you hold them inside or outside pension and other tax-deferred plans. Note whether the asset is tax-deferred, taxable, or tax-free (as with municipal bonds and many bond funds).

Stop here.

Look at your list and recall why, how, and from whom you acquired each asset. This is very revealing. Did you rely on your brother-in-law to advise you? Did you act on a tip? Did you rely on a broker, a hunch, or an inheritance? Were you satisfied with the result? If so, can it be repeated? Were you dissatisfied with the result? If so, be sure to avoid a repeat.

TIER-THREE INVESTMENTS

Next, write down your Tier-Three assets, which are your tangible assets and those that are speculative. Tier-Three investments include

Coins

Art

Antiques

Collectibles

Stamps

Limited partnerships in a business or real estate

Options to buy (call) commodities or to require others to buy (put) commodities

Gems

Commodities and futures contracts

Managed futures accounts

Foreign currency futures and options

Metals

Gold and precious metals

Any other speculation(s) you may have made

About each Tier-Three investment, ask yourself: What is it worth today? Is there a market for selling it? How did I acquire it? Can I repeat the process? About the duds, ask yourself: Can I liquidate and cut losses? Did I get a psychological benefit (investing in a play)? Should I take a tax loss and forget about it? These are adult decisions that you should make now. Clearing the decks and forgetting the past is all part of making up for lost time.

Did I forget something? Oh, your house. It's a little early to discuss the house in its full importance. For now, list its original purchase price, present value, and the outstanding mortgage. Do the same for any other real estate you own. If the property has a rent roll, list it and jot down the cost of running the building.

Now, review the list asset by asset. Have your goals changed since you acquired a certain asset? If so, does the asset still meet your goal? If not, or if the asset is a poor performer, place it on a "dump" list. Then make another list for the assets you would like to increase. Perhaps they are ones you already have. Perhaps they are ones suggested in the model portfolios (see Chapter 13). Put them on your "to buy" list. Selling failures and buying successes is called "asset repositioning." It's very healthy, and it's essential to making up for lost time.

Finally, add up the amount of assets you have in each tier, leaving out the value of your house. Express the amount you have in each tier as a percentage of your total assets. This is how you determine how your investments are allocated, also known as "asset allocation." For example, Bob and Jane's statement looks like this:

TOTAL ASSETS: $50,000 PLUS RESIDENCE

Tier One A: $5,000—savings, checking, money market
Tier One B: $10,000—government security income mutual fund
Tier Two: $25,000—assorted stocks and stock mutual funds
Tier Three: $10,000—speculation in real estate limited partnership

ASSET ALLOCATION

Tier One A: cash equivalents	10%
Tier One B: income	20%
Tier Two: growth	50%
Tier Three: speculation	20%

Knowing your asset allocation and the history behind your acquisitions is very important. Most likely, as you work through this book, you'll decide that you must liquidate some of your assets and exchange them for others in different tiers to meet your making-up-for-lost-time goals. Selling and exchanging (and sometimes taking a loss) can be scary. If you have a lot of Tier-Three tangibles, you may even have to sell your art or antiques. If you are resisting liquidating your assets, here's a wise word from Epictetus: "He is wise who does not grieve for the things which he has not, but rejoices for those which he has."

Some of your assets will be difficult to part with, particularly if like art they are tangible assets that give you a psychological benefit. Loser assets are difficult for some people to sell, because for them it's hard to admit defeat. Still other assets, especially real estate, are traditionally slower to liquidate, since most buyers need time to get financing.

Liquidating assets can cause emotional trouble. Don Steadman, a stockbroker-turned-cowboy at age forty-five, once told me, "Yuppies don't sell, they only buy." Aging yuppies that we are, we expect some resistance to liquidating, especially if our assets consist of art or crafts of value.

Those of you who need only to reposition assets, like stocks, bonds, and mutual funds, probably won't feel the resistance that those selling tangible assets will. Although many brokers tell me that some clients "fall in love with a stock" and can't sell, those with the biggest resistance problem are the people who own mostly art, real estate, and collectibles.

If you are one of them, to help yourself along, make a little chart like this one.

Item	Purchase Price	Market Value	Tax on Profit	OMDB*	ICGA†

---

*OMDB? This stands for "Over My Dead Body!" These are the things that you wouldn't sell even if you were starving, like Grandma's paisley shawl or the lithographs by the Russian artist you discovered. But indulge me. List them and see how much cash you could pocket if you really made the sale.
†ICGA? This stands for "It Can Go Anywhere." These things are the furniture and art with value that are really part of your home environment. Not for sale, even if you relocate. Just as well to keep these items—moving costs are less than the cost of refurnishing.

A WORD TO THE DEPRESSED

In Chapter 6 you will calculate the amount of assets you need to meet your retirement goal. You may be able to start from scratch and get there. If you have accumulated no assets at all, I will help you make sure that your goals are realistic enough to reach. Finally, if you are in debt and have a negative net worth, I offer you substantial information to help getting you out and getting you started.

Whatever your net worth today, keep in mind that if you stick with this program it will be greater tomorrow. Even if you are disappointed with your present net worth statement, look at it as your first step in making up for lost time.

NET WORTH STATEMENT

CASH AND EQUIVALENTS

Cash and Equivalents	When Acquired	From Whom Acquired (costs and commissions)	Purchase Price	Present Market Value	Taxable, Tax-exempt, or Tax-deferred	% of Your Total Portfolio	Current Yield	Meets Your Goal and Pace
Cash and savings account(s)								
Checking account(s)								
Money market(s)								
Cash value of insurance								
Gold bullion and coins								

NET WORTH STATEMENT

TIER-ONE ASSETS

	When Acquired	From Whom Acquired (costs, fees, commissions)	Purchase Price	Present Market Value	Taxable, Tax-exempt, or Tax-deferred	Total Returns in Past Calendar Year	Current Yield	Meets Your Goal and Pace
CDs								
CMOs								
Mutual bond funds								
Municipal bonds								
Unit trusts								
Treasuries								
Zero-coupon bonds (municipal, corporate, CMO)								
Fixed annuities								
Corporate bonds								
Foreign bonds								
Mortgages								
Other								

NET WORTH STATEMENT

TIER-TWO ASSETS

	When Acquired	From Whom Acquired (costs, fees, commissions)	Purchase Price	Present Market Value	Taxable, Tax-exempt, or Tax-deferred	% Growth in Last Calendar Year	Current Yield	Meets Your Goal and Pace
Common stocks								
Preferred stocks								
Variable annuities								
Investment real estate								
Royalties								
REITs								
Stock mutual funds								
Small C&D funds								
Growth funds								
Aggressive growth funds								
Global funds								
Universal life account								
Other								

NET WORTH STATEMENT

TIER-THREE ASSETS

	When Acquired	From Whom Acquired (costs, fees, commissions)	Purchase Price	Present Market Value	Taxable, Tax-exempt, or Tax-deferred	Potential for Gain	% of Investment That Can Be Lost	Meets Your Goal and Pace
Futures								
Options								
Metal/gold stocks								
Foreign currency								
Commodity mutual funds								
Art/antiques								
Limited partnerships								
Other								

NET WORTH STATEMENT

	Totals	Total Present Value
Cash and Equivalents		
Tier-One Assets		
Tier-Two Assets		
Tier-Three Assets		
Total Assets		

Asset Allocation	(% of your portfolio)
Cash and Equivalents	%
Tier-One Assets	%
Tier-Two Assets	%
Tier-Three Assets	%

THE NOBODY'S-BUSINESS-BUT-

MY-OWN BUDGET

The baby boomers . . . are reaching mid-life. The sense of unlim-

ited expectations that fueled their spending since the Sixties has

hit a plateau.

PETER SIRIS,
Barron's, March 1991

Everyone is telling you to *save! save! save!* But after years of consumer spending and locking in high fixed expenses, cutting back is
tough. It's also emotionally difficult to select a less expensive car
at forty than you drove at thirty, eat out fewer times a week, and
send your second child to public school when your firstborn went
to private school. But that is exactly what it takes to make up for
lost time. And if you spend less, you will be in keeping with the
times and with the rest of our generation.

For comfort, remember one of the major principles discussed
in Chapter 4: *You will never miss 10 percent of your income. Just
save it.*

I know that it's hard to take my word for it. So, for three months,
try the "pay yourself first experiment." Here's how it works.

Authorize your bank or money market fund to withdraw a
specific amount out of every paycheck or deposit you make in your
account. Have it deposited in a mutual fund that automatically
diversifies your savings. There you will receive a respectable return

on your contributions. Later on in the book you'll get a much more sophisticated understanding of these investments (see page 84 for investing in such a fund by calling an 800 number).

The purpose of the "pay yourself first experiment" is to get you into a consistent money-saving habit. Even if you are grossly in debt, follow the program, using instead of the fund a simple bank account. From this, you can withdraw amounts monthly to pay your creditors. When your ordeal is over, you can continue the saving habit for yourself. Even people in bankruptcy can start immediately to save, no matter how little.

For many of you, saving will come more easily than you can imagine if you do it on automatic pilot. *The key is never to miss a payment. Consider the saving plan a bill that must be paid every month. Don't hold off for any reason. If you miss a payment, the spell is broken and it may take you precious months to get back to doing it.*

By the second month you will discover that you can still pay your bills and you never miss the money. If saving frightens you because you worry that your lifestyle won't be as high or that your mortgage won't be paid, start small. Even $50 a month will prove you wrong and make you comfortable with ongoing saving. Whatever figure you choose, it must be planned and constant. In the retirement and college chapters of this book, you will learn to set future goals and calculate the amount you need to reach them in a given time. Eventually you will learn exactly the amount you must save to make up for lost time. For now, however, the amount is not as important as starting, and the discipline of continuing.

Even If You Think You Can't Budget, This Will Work for You

Budgets don't work for people over forty. In fact, they are so distasteful that they turn many people off from concentrating on their finances. That's why the Nobody's-Business-but-My-Own-Budget is not really a budget. It is a series of things you can do to spend less without budgeting.

First, evaluate what percentage of your income goes to various expenditures. On what is the lion's share of your income spent? If it's a flexible expense like eating out or buying clothes, you can change some of those old-fashioned eighties spending habits.

If the greatest proportion is a fixed expense like a car or mortgage debt, you can improve the situation by using the guidance on debt management in Chapter 20. If you have developed a very expensive financial "infrastructure," you may need a complete overhaul. For most home owners, the biggest expenditure goes to mortgage, home insurance, and home upkeep. This is normal, but if you are struggling with everything else, you may even decide it is wise to move. In the end you won't be sorry that you made a change in the present to arrive at the type of future that you long for.

To focus on what percent of your income goes where—to various fixed and flexible expenses—make a pie chart. This gives you a graphic look at your spending habits. Here's an example:

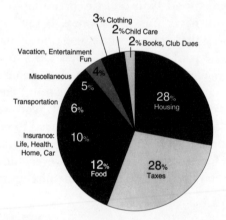

A pie chart can be a real eye-opener and an important way to point out imbalances in expenditures. Do your expenditures seem lopsided? Is one member of the family taking too much of the family income? Perhaps the chart reveals a high cost of an expendable luxury, for example, an expensive car that costs a lot to maintain and garage, or private exercise trainers when a club would do, or the late charges on debts because you are slow to pay.

These expenditures jump out at you when you see on paper the percent of your income they use up. Very soon your consciousness will be raised and your money habits will improve without following a budget.

Being super-aware of how you spend your money is, perhaps, the most critical habit change to learn after forty. Keeping your money and making it grow are now part of your daily work. Treat it that way, because someday the work will be finished and the money will go out and work for you.

Finally, if saving is not coming naturally to you, give up one big cost-consuming thing: stop eating out altogether, give up the country club, don't buy any clothes for a year.

THREE THINGS YOU CAN DO TO SAVE A FORTUNE

CUT UP YOUR CREDIT CARDS

I did. In 1987 I cut up my credit cards on the air during one of my broadcasts. My family's yearly expenditures went down more than $30,000 in the first year, and we never knew the difference. I also gave up lots of expensive lunches and clothes that didn't look so great anyway. Before the great cut-up, I earned a lot, I spent a lot, I saved nothing. After I shredded the cards, things changed drastically. I thought twice before I bought anything; I used cash and was aware of every purchase. I never made a budget, but I completely changed my habits. In Chapter 20, I'll give you hints on how to live with and without a credit card.

BECOME A TIGHTWAD

Some miserly people who don't spend money are miserable. But some tightwads are happy-go-lucky, like Amy Dacyczyn, author of *The Tightwad Gazette* (New York: Villard Books, 1993), and Marc Eisenson, author of *The Banker's Secret* (New York: Villard Books, 1980; reprinted). (Both edit newsletters of the same names as their books; see the Bibliography for information on how to subscribe). From couponing to bulk buying to getting all the refunds and rebates you deserve, some of you too may find that you enjoy the rewards of penny-pinching. Indeed, in the years I couldn't afford to save for my son's education, he saved $5,000 by keeping all the change his father and I threw around and by returning bottles and cans to get the deposit.

As I freely admit, I am by nature a squanderer not a saver. And here is a personal list of ways that even I can save money and have fun doing it.

- Buy generic drugs and other products. I was a lobbyist in Albany, New York, and Washington, DC, in favor of laws requiring pharmacies to post the names of generic drugs and their brand-name equivalents. The law was passed in most states.

- Shop at food co-ops or start one where you live. Food co-ops are the ultimate in bulk buying. For information, write to Co-op Directory Services, 919 21st Avenue South, Minneapolis, MN 55404.

- Buy directly from farmers. Even in New York City, there are farmer's markets where you can purchase fresh produce. A year's worth of fresh fruits organically or hydroponically grown can be contracted for at a fraction of supermarket or even greenmarket costs. The farmer is prepaid. Check your local papers at harvesttime for ads inviting you to visit farms. These "fun" visits can lead to economical arrangements for food.

- Barter. This is so important these days that it is becoming a viable business in itself. You can barter everything from baby-sitters to computers. For information on joining or starting an exchange, send a self-addressed, stamped envelope to the International Reciprocal Trade Association, 9513 Beach Mill Road, Great Falls, VA 22066.

- Rent clothes, cars, and any onetime items (Nancy Reagan rented some of her fancy ball dresses). Even expensive shoes are rentable today. For information, look in your phone book under the items you need, from party supplies to infant furniture.

- Use the library. When I lived in a commune as part of the research for this book, I got a full picture of how to use a library. Books, records, videos, 16-mm movies, play groups, senior activities, and even kids' birthday celebrations are available free or inexpensively through your local library.

- Stop smoking. This saves a bundle. My editor wants me to list cutting down on alcohol as well. The truth is I stopped smoking, but I still drink champagne. Do what suits you.

- Keep tax records. I guarantee that you are overpaying on your taxes if you don't. Even if you think you are being generous to yourself in figuring deductions, I bet you're cheating yourself.

- Watch your insurance dollar—see Chapter 21 to learn how.

- Spend money on home maintenance. It pays off in the long run. Or learn to do it yourself.

- Try spend-and-save cards. These cards give you rebates, discounts, or credit toward more purchases every time you buy from a store that is affiliated with them. They are a marketing tool to build buyer loyalty. Most charge a fee to join a club or get a card. At the time of this writing there is a big marketing push on these buying (not credit) cards. (I have been asked to act as spokesperson for two of them, but to retain my objectivity, I have decided not to.) They appear to be a good way to get rebates and save costs as long as you intend to make the purchase anyway. One card called Start contributes 6 percent of your yearly purchases from a variety of stores to a Metropolitan Life Annuity in your name. For information, call Horizon Marketing, 516–621–4653.

DO SERIOUS DOWNSCALING

When you take a look at where you would like to be in the future, you may find that you have built such a burdensome infrastructure that ordinary saving measures just can't get you where you want to go. Or perhaps your job and earnings have changed.

If you were a highly paid executive in the eighties, you might well be starting out as a free-lance consultant in the nineties. If you were a real estate professional, you may have had to retool completely. Yet the cost of your house, private schooling, and social events keep you frightened and inflexible. In *Fear of Falling* (New York: Pantheon, 1989), her study of the middle class's earnings' crisis, Barbara Ehrenreich paints a graphic picture of how we try to hold on to old spending habits and keep up appearances when our earnings and expectations decline.

If this is you, you may have to completely downscale in order to make up for lost time. This often entails moving, changing schools, and sometimes changing friends. It's tough work. But it is the ultimate in financial liberation. I personally did major surgery on my lifestyle. And I can attest that without exception every sacrifice was worthwhile.

CALCULATING FINANCIAL

SUCCESS WITH A SHARP PENCIL

If you can earn 10 percent on your investment and wish to achieve a $100,000 goal, it will take $14,890 invested every year in a lump sum to reach that goal in five years; $5,704 per year to reach it in ten years; $924.37 per year to reach it in twenty-five years, and only $205 per year to reach it in forty years.

ADRIANE G. BERG,
Your Wealth-Building Years

If you know your goal, you are very likely to meet it. The trouble is that most of us want "the most money we can make." That leaves us with no sensible measure of success. If we can't measure success, we can't achieve it. This was the heartbreak of the eighties. Many of us could have achieved reasonable financial goals merely by selling appreciated real estate or other tangibles. But most of us missed the boat. We never set a target clear enough to know when it had been reached. Let's get a bead on our goals right now.

GET A QUICK FIX ON YOUR FINANCIAL GOALS

Presume an investment yield of 10 percent. This is realistic under the investment system you'll learn in this book. This retirement savings chart shows you how much you must save each year in order to accumulate between $25,000 and $750,000 in a nest egg, assuming a yield of 10 percent. For example, to meet a nest egg goal of $200,000 in ten years, you must save $12,549 per year.

		Years Until Retirement							
		5	*10*	*15*	*20*	*25*	*30*	*35*	*40*
	$25,000	$4,095	$1,569	$787	$436	$254	$152	$92	$5
	50,000	8,190	3,137	1,574	873	508	304	184	11
Nest	100,000	16,380	6,275	3,147	1,746	1,017	608	369	22
Egg	150,000	24,570	9,412	4,721	2,619	1,525	912	553	33
Goal	200,000	32,759	12,549	6,295	3,492	2,034	1,216	738	45
	300,000	49,139	18,824	9,442	5,238	3,050	1,824	1,107	67
	500,000	81,899	31,373	15,737	8,730	5,084	3,040	1,845	1,13
	750,000	122,848	47,059	23,605	13,095	7,626	4,559	2,767	1,69

By studying this chart you gain an appreciation of disciplined savings and of the importance of time in accumulating wealth. Clearly, the longer and the more you save, the greater the financial result. To illustrate, here is a quiz question for you.

Investor A begins an investment program of $2,000 a year at age twenty-seven and saves for eight years to age thirty-four (total investment $16,000). He makes no further investments. After that, time and compound interest work for him.

Investor B begins his program at age thirty-five, saving $2,000 a year for thirty years until age sixty-five (total investment $60,000).

Investor C begins to invest at age forty and continues for twenty-five years until he reaches sixty-five. He invests $3,000 a year, 50 percent more than the others (total investment $75,000).

Who has more money at age sixty-five?

By age sixty-five, their respective savings look like this:

Investor A—$439,008

Investor B—$361,887

Investor C—$324,545

To catch up to Investor A, Investor C would have to make an annual deposit of more than double that of Investor A, and would have to save for longer than three times the number of years (twenty-five for C and only eight for A).

I give you this example to encourage you to start saving as soon as possible. Time is a powerful investment tool. If you have very little time before "G Day" (goal date), you'll have to set a reasonable, and perhaps diminished, goal or move up the date.

IF YOU ARE CLOSE TO YOUR GOAL DATE, SET A GOAL AT WHAT YOU NEED, NOT WHAT YOU WANT

In Chapter 12, you will be asked to estimate your retirement needs. You'll set yourself a "retirement salary" that your money must earn for you. This retirement savings chart adds an inflation factor of 4 percent into your calculation. It focuses you. Staying with the 10 percent investment yield, it shows you the amount of assets needed at retirement in five to forty years in order to generate from $5,000 to $50,000 in yearly income.

Years Until Retirement

Retirement Income Annually Generated	5	10	15	20	25	30	35	40
$5,000	$60,833	$74,012	$90,047	$109,556	$133,292	$162,170	$197,304	$240,051
$10,000	121,665	148,024	180,094	219,112	266,584	324,340	394,609	480,102
$15,000	182,498	222,037	270,142	328,668	399,875	486,510	591,913	720,153
$20,000	243,331	296,049	360,189	438,225	533,167	648,680	789,218	960,204
$25,000	304,163	370,061	450,236	547,781	666,459	810,849	986,522	1,200,255
$30,000	364,996	444,073	540,283	657,337	799,751	973,019	1,183,827	1,440,306
$40,000	486,661	592,098	720,377	876,449	1,066,335	1,297,359	1,578,436	1,920,408
$50,000	608,326	740,122	900,472	1,095,562	1,332,918	1,621,699	1,973,044	2,400,510

Let's say you choose to retire in fifteen years with an annual income of $40,000. Your goal is to accumulate $720,377. Now look again at the chart on page 58. You will see that, starting from scratch, you must invest $23,605 each year at 10 percent to accumulate $750,000, a bit more than your goal.

If in retirement you can live on $10,000 less a year ($30,000), you'll need a nest egg of $540,283. That requires an annual savings of approximately $15,737. Go back and forth a few times between the two charts on pages 58 and 60. Set different retirement salary goals and retirement dates. Then look at the chart on page 60 to see how much you must accumulate and the chart on page 58 to see the annual savings you need to reach that amount. Don't be alarmed by these preliminary figures; they presume that you have accumulated no assets whatsoever. Keep reading.

GET AN IDEA OF HOW MUCH THE MONEY YOU ALREADY HAVE ACCUMULATED WILL GROW BY THE TARGET DATE

Many of you will not be starting from ground zero. You may have to make up for lost time, but most likely you already have managed to save a bit, or contribute to a pension plan. Or perhaps your real estate has maintained substantial equity. This chart shows you how far toward your goal you have already come.

			Years Until Retirement				
5	10	15	20	25	30	35	40
1.61	2.59	4.18	6.73	10.83	17.45	28.10	45.26

Assume you make 10 percent on your investment and plan to retire in ten years. Multiply your current assets by 2.59 to see how they will grow by the target date. Take the value at retirement of your present assets as calculated from this chart and subtract this amount from the total nest egg you will need to generate retirement income. Then figure the amount you must save each year from now until your goal date.

For example, Bill and Hillary are forty years old and they plan to work until age sixty-five. They have saved $30,000 in a pension plan. They want to retire with $50,000 of income assuming 4 percent inflation.

With a 10 percent return, the $30,000 will grow by a multiple of 10.83 (see the chart on page 61), so their present assets will be worth $324,900 at retirement. They will need a total of $1,332,918 in assets to generate the targeted income (see the chart on page 60). Given the $324,900 they will have by retirement date, they still need to accumulate more than $1,000,000 dollars in the next twenty-five years. It seems impossible, but they can get close to their goal with annual savings of $10,168 (see the chart on page 58). That will bring them $100,000.

Wow! A couple, already forty years of age, who have saved only $30,000 between them can still retire as millionaires! Let's look at the factors that make this possible. You will see that it's not magic.

First, all the figures are based on tax-deferred investing. They must have a pension program to which they can make contributions.

Second, they are saving as they never saved before. Within four and a half years they will save as much as they did in the first twenty years of their work life.

You can do it too. Naturally, your own goals and expectations will be the criteria for your calculations. In Chapter 12, you will calculate with precision the assets you have, the income you target, the retirement date you select, and the investment yield you will shoot for.

A final point: In order to reach their goal, Bill and Hillary are earning 10 percent on their investments. That means keeping a keen eye on investment yield and being willing to reposition investments that don't make the grade. Let's read more about how the Three-Tier system can help you earn 10 percent and a lot more.

Drexel Burnham Is Dead and I Don't Feel So Good Myself:

A Primer of Investment Choices to Make Up for Lost Time

THE THREE-TIER METHOD:
MAKING UP FOR LOST TIME BY
TURNING YOUR INVESTMENT
STRATEGY UPSIDE DOWN

"You are old, Father William," the young man said; . . . "And yet

you incessantly stand on your head—"

LEWIS CARROLL,
Alice's Adventures in Wonderland

To make up for lost time, start thinking in terms of three tiers of investments. When you created your net worth statement, in Chapter 4, you categorized your existing investments into the following three tiers:

Tier-One investments are interest-bearing, guaranteed, and date-targeted. Examples are Treasury notes, certificates of deposit, and corporate and government bonds with a maturity date that will coincide with your target goal date. A prime example of a Tier One are so-called zero-coupon bonds, which guarantee you a certain sum at a specified date. Tier Ones are *planned, steady, and targeted.*

Tier-Two growth investments have no specific maturity dates and fewer guarantees. These assets include common and preferred stocks, many types of mutual funds, and some real estate. Tier

Twos are *market-sensitive, actively bought and sold, and performance-oriented.*

Tier-Three investments are speed-investing techniques to make money fast. They are speculative investments like commodities, options, metals, and certain international investments. They are characterized by any investment that uses "leverage." This means that you can buy and sell a large portfolio with a payment of far less than the cost of 100 percent of the investment. If you succeed, you make a profit on the entire investment as if you paid for all of it initially. If you lose, you lose only the amount of your payment. Tier Threes are *opportunity-oriented, leveraged, risky, and fast-moving.*

Other Tier-Three investments are tangibles like art, coins, and antiques. For many of us there is a fine line between these tangibles and outright luxury items. They do have place in making up for lost time. Certainly, there is money to be made in art, coins, stamps, and the like, but only if you are a buyer and a trader, not a buyer and a keeper.

To Make Up for Lost Time, Stand Your Portfolio on Its Head

If you are like most of us, you invested first in the things you could see, touch, and enjoy: houses, furniture, perhaps art, and so forth. Second, you invested in things you thought would make you quick money: a tip on a penny stock, a junk bond with a high interest rate. Only lastly, if at all, did you calculate a goal with precision and invest solely to achieve that goal.

The reasons for this typical pattern of investing are rooted in the American Dream itself: Our net worth and our self-worth get confused. Buying things helps us feel good. It's so easy to buy, and so complicated to invest. Further, tangible buying can often be done with credit cards or mortgages or seller financing. We can make impulse purchases. We can have it now, pay for it later.

Whether you are more heavily invested in Tier-One, Tier-Two, or Tier-Three investments usually depends on factors that have little to do with good investing and more to do with convenience. Most people buy what's offered. If a bank is selling certificates of deposit, you buy them. If your brother-in-law has introduced you to a persistent broker, you may own stocks or partnerships.

In creating your net worth statement, you explored how you arrived at your present portfolio. If the method was based purely on reaching a goal and investing for it, you probably don't need to make up for lost time, unless you have suffered a spectacular loss or a career change. Most of us have not been goal-oriented, however.

How to Build the Right Three-Tier Portfolio

An essential element of making up for lost time is the proper allocation of your assets among the three tiers. What is "proper" is dictated by your goals, how fast you want to reach them and how far along toward them you already are.

Selecting investments from the three tiers is like designing a nutrition plan. There are guidelines, but no one menu is right for everyone. In fact, menus must be adjusted even for the same person from time to time. After you have made your first allocation toward your goal, check up on it a minimum of every six months (more often is even better) to make sure that its overall performance is sufficient to meet your goal.

Tier-One investments are best made under these circumstances:

1. You are within five years of retirement or another goal date, you are very close to meeting your goal, and you are very conservative, wishing to avoid both principal and interest rate risk.

2. You are very close to the goal date but very far from meeting your goal, and you are willing to select a more minimal goal, as long as you can be guaranteed success in meeting it.

3. You have a very long time to meet your goal, you are very risk-averse, and you prefer protection of principal as opposed to inflation protection. (This approach is used least by those

trying to make up for lost time, as it usually does not accumulate wealth fast enough to meet most goals.)

Tier-Two investments are best made under these circumstances:

1. You are ten years or more from your goal date.
2. You are near your goal date or have been able to reach it,
   and you are willing to risk some principal to exceed your
   goal.

Tier-Three investments are best made under these
circumstances:

1. You have reached or will surely reach your goal, and you
   want to risk a small amount of capital for very high potential
   returns.
2. You find it impossible to reach your goal, you have the temperament to take a very risky chance at achieving your goal,
   and you are willing to risk losing a portion of what you have
   achieved if you fail.

As an overall approach, Tier-Two growth investments work best
to make up for lost time. The longer you have until your goal date,
the more heavily your portfolio should favor Tier Twos.

Let's look at a theoretical couple with $50,000 to invest at age
forty and twenty-five years to retirement. They could put nearly
100 percent of their assets in Tier Twos in this way:

10 percent in aggressive growth stocks

25 percent in growth stocks

5 percent in international stocks

50 percent in larger or mid-capitalization (often thought of as
blue-chip) stocks

10 percent in mixed assets (with a fractional amount in Tier-
One bonds)

Now let's look at the same couple ten years later. As their goal date gets closer, let's say seven to five years or less away, they begin to decrease the Tier Twos and replace them with Tier Ones. The rapidity with which they do this depends on the weight they give to rising inflation (Tier Twos work best protecting the buying power of the dollar in inflationary times), the importance they place on safety and predictability (Tier Ones work best for predictability), and/or their desire to exceed their goal or to secure it (Tier Twos for the former, Tier Ones for the latter).

Tier-Three investments are really speculations. They come in as an extra kick to the couple's potential wealth or as insurance against a high inflation rate (if the tangibles are metals or real estate).

In the next three chapters you will be introduced to the vast number of different investments you can choose in each tier. Don't be intimidated, and always remember the "Blue Suit Theory of Investing" (page 33): Don't be frozen into inaction by the numerous investment choices there are or by the fear of making an imperfect allocation. If you are a few percentage points more heavily invested in any tier than you should be, you can adjust it as you go along. Being more or less in the right pattern is enough.

The next three chapters tell you the details on investment selection. Skim this heavy stuff. Then reread sections when you get down to making your choices.

Choosing the Best Tier-One Investments to Make Up for Lost Time

Income is traditionally the most important reason people own bonds. . . . They also offer more security than most common stocks.

NANCY DUNNAN,
Guide to Investments

The primary purpose of Tier Ones is to generate income after retirement, so they will be a small percentage of our making-up-for-lost-time portfolio. This percentage will increase as we get closer to our goal and begin to convert Tier Twos into Tier Ones for greater financial stability and a definite income stream. There is one Tier-One investment, however, that works well even years before retirement or reaching a target goal: zero-coupon bonds. To understand them fully, you must have a good grasp of Tier-One investing in general.

As a side benefit, you will be able to help your parents with their income-investing needs. Further, the average short-term investment yield of a Tier One over the past four decades has been approximately 5.5 percent. Today it's only 2.5 percent. Watch for yields above 5.5 percent and lock them in when they come your way. For example, in the seventies, a 19 percent thirty-year Treasury bill was marketed. Few people bought it because they were not aware of the extraordinary return this ensured. What a lost opportunity to MUFLT! So let's understand Tier Ones.

Tier Ones Are Not Investments!

When you make Tier-One investments, you lend your money to various institutions in return for their obligation to pay you back with interest. These "borrowing institutions" are usually banks, municipalities, corporations, or the federal government. If you view Tier-One investments as loans from you to them, it becomes easy to judge one loan arrangement compared to another. The factors to be evaluated in each case are

1. The amount of return on your money (always partially a function of the maturity date)
2. The safety of your principal
3. The guarantee of return on your money

Let's examine each factor more closely.

THE AMOUNT OF RETURN ON YOUR MONEY

Naturally, you want a Tier-One investment that offers a high return on your money, and there are three types of returns to consider.

Simple Interest

Bank accounts and certificates of deposit (CDs) often pay a stated amount of interest each year. This is known as simple interest. You can find the amount you will earn each year by multiplying the principal by the interest rate of the investment.

Bonds of all types have a coupon rate. This is the same as simple interest in bank securities.

Compound Interest

Bank securities often pay you interest on the interest you have earned. This is called compound interest. If interest is compounded daily, you earn more interest on the interest calculated each day. If interest is compounded quarterly, you must wait until each quarter to be credited with the additional interest that in turn earns interest. The more frequent the compounding, the higher your return.

Current Yield

The return you receive on bonds can be different from the coupon rate if you sell before maturity. The current yield is the coupon rate divided by the present price of the bond (not the price you paid for it). Since the bond market value fluctuates constantly, current yield will vary frequently, just as a stock price does. You are not interested in the current yield unless you plan to buy and sell bonds as the market changes. For the most part, your plan is to buy and hold. Therefore, the constant fluctuations in current yield shouldn't affect your Tier-One strategy.

Yield to Maturity   This term describes the earnings to be had if the bond is held to maturity and if every penny of interest is invested at the market rate of interest at the time you bought the bond. Yield to maturity is a good measure of return on your money for a Tier-One investment if you plan to receive and reinvest interest each month. Make sure that in quoting the yield to maturity, the broker takes into account any premium above par (face value) you will pay.

One caution. The yield to maturity is only a ballpark number. You can't be sure that you will be able to reinvest income at the same rate as the bond pays for the entire life of the bond. After all, bonds give fixed rates; your reinvestment vehicles may not.

For example, if you deposit and accumulate interest in a money market account until you have enough to buy another bond, the money market and the new bond will probably have interest rates different from the original bond. If you deposit the interest in an income mutual fund, the amount earned from that will be different once again.

Even though yield to maturity does not give you a precise calculation of what you will derive from the investment, it is still a very good measure of return on your money for the Tier-One investments that you plan to hold to maturity.

Total Return   Another popular method of quoting yield is "total return." Total return is measured by calculating both the annual interest rate and the gain or loss in principal when you sell the bond. Therefore, most of the time, total return will be calculated based on the par (face) value of the bond.

Sometimes, however, bonds—which usually sell "at par" (another word for $1,000 per bond)—have such a low interest coupon that they sell at a discount: i.e., at $950. At other times, the interest is so high as compared with other bonds that they sell at a premium "above par": $1,030. If you buy a non-par bond, total return must take the loss or gain in principal into consideration. Your broker will make the calculation for you.

THE SAFETY OF YOUR PRINCIPAL

The safety of your principal (that is, your guarantee of repayment) is weaker or stronger depending upon the borrower. You pay for a stronger repayment guarantee in the form of receiving lower interest, or total return. A corporate bond is only as good as the creditworthiness of the corporation. A Treasury bill is as solid as the federal government itself. Accordingly, corporate bond interest rates are usually higher than interest on Treasuries.

Further, safety is affected by the type of collateral securing your bond. Public utility bonds are really mortgages. The bonds are secured by the property of the company. Corporate bonds are debentures. There is no specific collateral securing your principal, just the creditworthiness of the company itself. Equipment (like railroad rolling stock, or airplanes) trust securities have specific collateral. Subordinated bonds are bonds that are not secured with collateral; moreover, there are other creditors who will collect before you will in the event of a default.

Municipal bonds can be revenue, general obligation, or project bonds. A revenue bond pays from the revenue collected from the operation of the bridge, tunnel, or other facility built with your borrowed money. If that endeavor fails, so can your payback. A general obligation bond is a liability of the municipality that is paid from all funds, including collected taxes. It is the safest of all such bonds. Finally, a project bond, the riskiest, pays only from the profits gleaned from a special project, i.e., a convention center.

Moody's and Standard & Poor's are two companies that rate the safety of bonds. S&P rates the safest bonds as AAA; Moody's uses Aaa (both spoken of as "triple A"-rated). Never buy a bond without knowing its rating. Very low rated bonds are often called "junk bonds": little safety, high interest. These are not suitable Tier-One investments.

Some bonds are insured. You will get a return of about .25 percent less as a trade-off to the insurance factor. My approach is to buy high-rated, uninsured bonds. Sometimes, however, a well-rated bond is also insured. If other factors are to your liking, i.e., if the maturity date falls near your goal date, buy it.

Treasuries are not rated, as they have no default risk.

Bank deposits, including certificates of deposit, are not rated, since up to $100,000 is insured by the Federal Deposit Insurance Corporation (FDIC). However, since the Savings and Loan (S&L) crisis, many investors are checking the safety of their banks. You can do this by calling Veribanc, 1–800–837–4226, a service that as of this writing charges $10 to give you banks' ratings. You can check rates with Rate-Fax, The Bradshaw Financial Network. Write to The Bradshaw Financial Network, Suite 13, 253 Channing Way, San Rafael, CA 94903–2605.

THE GUARANTEE OF RETURN ON YOUR MONEY

The safety features just discussed all relate to your chances of getting back all the interest and the principal that you anticipate. Some Tier-One investments guarantee the principal but not the amount of the return. Others guarantee neither but have a history of good returns.

These investments include utility stocks that pay regular dividends, and stock certificates of deposit (banks and brokerage houses guarantee the principal; the interest you receive is measured by the rise and fall of a selected stock index). These are really hybrids of both Tier-One and Tier-Two investments. They are generally marketed to investors looking for Tier Ones. In making up for lost time, they are not my favorites. They give you neither the chance for growth of principal that Tier Twos do nor the safe predictability of Tier Ones. They are excellent for post- and pre-retirees who want to diversify into different kinds of income-producing assets. That's not you until several years from now.

TAXABILITY OF TIER-ONE INVESTING

Tier-One investing has a different long-term result depending on the taxability of the interest earned. Interest may be taxable, tax-deferred, or tax-exempt. Under the Internal Revenue Code, you must report earned income from Tier-One investments even if you reinvest and do not spend the money. This is the rule of "constructive receipt."

Fortunately (and especially for those trying to make up for lost time), you can defer paying tax on earned income if the Tier One is one owned in a pension program. Chapter 16 will give you the rules for tax-deferred pensions and private annuities.

It is critical that as many Tier-One investments as possible be owned this way to take advantage of the extra boost to wealth accumulation that tax deferral brings.

Some Tier Ones, like municipal and bond funds, are completely tax-exempt. As an incentive to buy their bonds and notes, states and municipalities do not charge you income tax on the interest you receive. The federal government does not tax you on such bonds because of a Constitutional restraint. Hence you receive income "triple-tax-free."

Be aware, however, that in order to escape state and municipal taxes you must reside in the jurisdiction that issued the bond. For example, if you live in New Jersey and buy a New York bond, you will pay tax on the interest income on your New Jersey state income tax return. Also be aware that Treasury bills, notes, and bonds are federally taxed, but you will never pay state or municipal tax on the income, no matter where you live.

Because of these tax advantages, municipal bonds often pay less interest than other competing Tier-One investments. Treasuries often pay less because they are partially tax-free and very safe. It's easy to tell whether you are better off with a higher-interest taxable investment or a lower-interest tax-free investment. Just use this formula.

100 − your tax bracket × the interest rate = the after-tax interest in your pocket

For example, a municipality offers an 8 percent interest rate tax-free. A corporation offers a 10 percent corporate bond, which is taxable. Which is best if safety is not a factor?

If you are in the 15 percent tax bracket, using the formula for the taxable bond

100 − 15 = 85 × 10% = 8.5%

you get 8.5 percent after taxes with the corporate bond, compared to 8 percent with the municipal bond. The corporate bond is the better investment even though it is taxable.

If you are in the 33 percent bracket, however, using the formula for the taxable bond

100 − 33 = 67 × 10% = 6.7%

you get only 6.7 percent after taxes with the corporate bond, compared to 8 percent with the municipal bond. Here the municipal bond is the better investment.

This is why, traditionally, higher earners paying higher taxes like municipal bonds as a Tier-One investment.

A FINAL WORD OF CAUTION

If you do buy Tier Ones because they help you target a specific goal at a specific time, be aware that bonds and other Tier Ones may be "callable," that is, redeemed prior to the maturity date. This happens when interest rates fall and the bonds can be resold with lower rates. This will play havoc with your plan.

Some bonds even have a "sinking fund," an escrow account with moneys designated to redeem the bonds at intervals. This is a safety feature for which you will pay by getting a lower return. Such bonds are not good for Tier-One investing. You are paying for a feature you'd rather avoid. A bond with a sinking fund is subject to a periodic lottery. If your bond "wins," it gets redeemed early. Just what you would like to avoid!

ZERO-COUPON BONDS—THE PERFECT TIER-ONE INVESTMENT TO MAKE UP FOR LOST TIME

Zero-coupon bonds are available as municipal bonds, Treasury bonds, corporate bonds, collateralized mortgage obligations (CMOs), and FICOs (Federal Insurance Corporation Organization) issued by the Treasury to bail out the S&Ls. All federal government zeros are very safe. Some Treasury zeros are bought directly from the issuer. Other zeros, called Lions, Cats, and Tigers, are actually obligations of the brokerage house from which you buy them. They are collateralized by the Treasury bond, but you are not buying the bond itself. You are buying the brokerage house's promise to pay, backed by Treasuries as collateral.

Here's how zeros work.

Years ago, a bond actually had little coupons attached. The coupons could be removed once a month and taken to any bank that would redeem them for cash. This was called "clipping coupons."

Today, bonds can be separated into principal and interest after they are issued. The brokerage house can sell the right to monthly interest as one investment, and the right to collect principal at maturity as another investment. The investment that bestows only the right to get the principal or face value of the bond is called a "zero-coupon bond." Get it? Since the zero pays no immediate interest, its return is calculated based on an internal rate of growth compounded semi-annually. Always check this figure by asking the broker for the total return that you can expect of your zero and its yield to maturity.

When you buy a zero you will find that you are buying it at a discount below its par ($1,000 per bond) value. So, you might pay $500 for a discount zero coupon that pays you back $1,000 in face value in ten years. The amount of the discount figures into your return, but it is not the ultimate buying criterion. Keep your focus on total return and yield to maturity.

Unless they are issued by municipalities, zeros are taxable each year even though you do not get paid your profit until the maturity date. This means that you will pay a tax each year on a sum called "the accreted value." This sum is calculated by your broker, and a statement is sent to you before tax time. You will defer all tax if you own the zero in your pension plan.

The problem of a bond being prepaid by the issuer ("called") is particularly severe with zeros. That is because the rate of growth of the bond accelerates as the maturity date approaches. Bond issuers have a high incentive to pay off before you are entitled to the high growth.

Keeping all this in mind, I am of the opinion that the very best Tier-One combination is a zero-coupon bond with a good total return, and call protection owned by you in a tax-deferred pension.

WHEN CHOOSING TIER ONES

Judge every Tier One by its safety, return, guarantee, and tax effect. Make up a simple sheet like this one to analyze and compare Tier Ones.

Comparison Sheet for Choosing Tier-One Investments

1. Total return:
2. Maturity date:
3. Safety rating:
4. Call protection:
5. Other features (insurance sinking fund):
6. Tax consequence:

CHOOSING THE BEST TIER-TWO

INVESTMENTS TO MAKE UP FOR

LOST TIME

I love mutual funds because they're so easy as well as smart. Anyone

can learn enough to buy a good one.

JANE BRYANT QUINN,
Making the Most of Your Money

The mainstay of Two-Tier investing is common stock. There are
two ways of buying stock: (1) buying shares in individual companies
through a broker, and (2) buying shares in mutual funds that own
a diversity of stocks from a licensed salesperson or directly from
the fund.

Choose individual shares if you can spend a lot of time managing
your own portfolio, or if you can find a high-performing stock
portfolio manager to do it for you. If you have little time or professional help, opt for the mutual fund. If you become more immersed
in financial news, and a stock strategy or a particular company
interests you, you can then add individual investments to your
mutual funds.

The fact is, however, that even with time and help, it is best to
go with mutual funds if the amount you have to invest is $50,000
or less. With just a few individual stocks, you can't achieve the

diversification that leads to the investment pace you need to make up for lost time.

Tier-Two Investments with Mutual Funds

Mutual funds are companies that pool your money with that of other investors to buy many types of securities. When you invest, you receive a share in the fund purchased at its net asset value (NAV). NAV is calculated by dividing the total asset value of the fund minus liabilities by the number of outstanding shares. NAV is recalculated each day. When you sell at a profit, you are selling at a higher NAV than when you bought. You may also make a profit by receiving income, dividends, and capital gains from a fund.

Each company offers different funds with different investment purposes. Some funds are Tier One, others are Tier Three. For those making up for lost time, it is the Tier-Two funds that are the most useful. This is so because wise Tier-Two investing requires great diversification, constant reinvestment of gains, constant contribution of more capital, ability to own investments in a pension fund or tax-deferred vehicle, and good management. Mutual funds provide all this.

The best Tier-Two funds for your purpose will concentrate on stocks with long-term prospects for appreciation. Since, at this writing, there are 4,300 mutual funds to choose from and still counting, here are some thoughts on making a selection.

Read Before You Buy

In the vast universe of material on investing with mutual funds, I would target the following best reads:

Guide to Mutual Funds 1994 (or the most current edition) (New York: McGraw-Hill Inc.). Available in bookstores, this gives

you an overview of mutual fund investing and rates a thousand
funds.

Investor's Guide to Low-Cost Mutual Funds, which comes in a Combination Kit along with *Directing Your Own Mutual Fund Investments*. Available from Mutual Fund Education Alliance,
Suite 120, 1900 Erie Street, Kansas City, MO 64116.

More pricey is *The Handbook of No-Load Fund Investors*. Available
from The No-Load Fund Investor, P.O. Box 318, Irvington,
NY 10533

As you purchase mutual funds, you may well begin to pay
attention to the articles about them in financial magazines. These
articles rate funds, provide gossip about fund managers, and offer
predictions about future results. *Forbes, Money, U.S. News & World
Report*, and *Worth* are a few of the many magazines that rate funds.
Morningstar, Inc. is the most comprehensive monthly report and is
available in the reference section of your library.

In fact, reports are proliferating so fast (Value Line is starting
a service even as I write) that we need a report to explain how the
reports rate a fund! To make up for lost time, use a rating system
that gives high marks for consistency over time rather than performance during one year. To make money management easy, plan to
buy and hold. So look for the funds that did well during all markets,
even if they were never number one, rather than big hitters during
certain types of markets.

To Simplify Your Investment Choice, Familiarize Yourself with a "Family of Funds"

Many mutual fund companies carry a line of funds, called a
"family of funds," each with its own investment purpose. The
companies allow you to switch among the funds at will; sometimes
there is a $5 to $25 fee each time you switch. *Weisberger's Investment
Companies Service*, which can be found in the reference section of
your library, lists funds by investment objective, the type of investments they hold, and their results.

Once You Have Selected One or Two "Families," Focus on the Tier-Two Choices Within Them

Here's how to dig in and know about your Two-Tier investment choices with mutual funds.

- Know the fund manager. A team of investment managers selects the actual investments. Often, one person is the wunderkind. Some funds are even named for the manager. If you buy a personality-based fund, hope that the guru doesn't retire, and follow the stories in the financial press.
- Buy funds that fit your Tier-Two investment purpose. You'll find the funds' purpose stated in the prospectus. Tier-Two funds are growth funds, aggressive growth funds, global equity funds, and asset allocation funds which switch from cash to equities and even include Tier-One investments. (Go for asset allocation funds only when you are very near your goal date.)
- Rank the funds in order of their risk level and match them to your level of risk tolerance. In general, the rank from least risky to riskiest is

  Asset allocation funds

  Growth funds

  Global equity funds

  Aggressive growth funds

  Small caps funds

  Sector funds (riskiest because they invest in only one sector of the economy and don't diversify much)
- Check the price/earnings ratio (P/E) of the stocks the fund holds. Average-risk stocks have a P/E of about 19. *The Wall Street Journal* publishes Standard & Poor's P/E for stocks. Or you can either call the fund to find out the P/E of its holdings or look up individual stocks it owns in the newspaper. A change in a fund's P/E shows a change in its risk philosophy. A lower P/E can mean a lower-risk philosophy.

- Make a list of two or three funds in categories that are of interest to you. Read the books and financial magazines I mentioned that rate performance. Look at performance over five years to the present. If the fund has done well over time, but had its best years early on, it may be going downhill.
- Some funds require a minimum investment. These will eliminate themselves if you can't afford the minimum.
- Look for service and convenience. Call the fund's 800 number. If you get through and the person is polite, that's a plus. Find out if you can buy and sell by both mail and telephone, how quickly orders are processed, and whether you can automatically reinvest dividends. Most funds are pretty efficient at doing these things, but if you find a dud, cut it dead. If you use a financial planner, he or she will help make decisions and allocations.

If you have trouble making a selection, here are two simple choices that work:

1. Buy an index fund. An index fund invests in all the stocks followed by a market index, like Dow Jones. One type follows the bond market (Tier-One investing), the other follows the stock market (Tier-Two investing). Over the years, you'll do as well as any average investor without putting in a lot of hard work.
2. Buy a fund that invests solely in other funds. These invest in a variety of Tier-Two funds for lots of diversification.

Finally, to become a real connoisseur, subscribe to a mutual fund newsletter. These are advertised in most financial newspapers and magazines. *Mutual Fund Values*, published by Morningstar Inc., 53 West Jackson Boulevard, Chicago, IL 60604, is a good bet. Many mutual funds will give you Morningstar ratings and Lipper ratings (another rating service) if you ask them.

Pay Close Attention to Commissions, Fees, and Costs

The costs of purchasing and maintaining a fund are very important in its selection, and often the subject of much controversy. First, I'll give you the facts, then I'll give you my opinion.

You will encounter three types of costs with a mutual fund: loads, fees, and operating expenses. Loads are commissions paid to a salesperson. A front-end load is one paid out of the investment you make when you make it. It is a sales charge that can range from 3 to 8.5 percent (you can get a break if you invest large sums). It is illegal for the salesperson to give you deals like rebates, however. So, don't deal with people who offer them.

Some funds charge a load every time you reinvest dividends. Others charge a load when you sell (a back-end load, or redemption fee). Yet others impose a back-end load only if you sell within a short period of time. These charges are between 3 and 4 percent. They may be taken from the initial amount invested or from the total amount you withdraw.

What are known as 12 B-1 loads are small amounts (between 0.25 and 1 percent) charged each year. They can go on forever, or stop when you have held a fund for a cerain number of years. Some 12 B-1 funds don't charge 12 B-1 loads unless some contingency occurs (for example, if you withdraw a high percentage of your investment soon after you've made it).

In short, there are load, no-load, low-load, 12 B-1-, and back-end-load funds. The salesperson for load funds and the 800 number person for no-load funds will give you the information on all of this, as will the prospectus.

Besides commissions, there are also management fees, accounting fees, and start-up fees. All of these expenses and fees (but not the commissions) are computed and reported to you in comparison to the total assets held in the fund. This is called the expense ratio. Expense ratios can run from from 0.5 to 3 percent. Examples of what they may be are found in a fund's prospectus.

To sort all this out quickly, here's a checklist to use with your broker, financial planner, 800 number person, or when you are reviewing a fund's prospectus:

WHAT TO ASK ABOUT MUTUAL FUND FEES

- What class of share am I buying?
  A Shares—Front-end load
  B Shares—Commission recouped over time, then converted
  to A shares
  C & D—(Level Load) Annual percentage to broker each
  year
- What is the up-front sales-charge load?
- What is the redemption fee (back-end load)?
- What is the load on reinvested dividends?
- What is the load or "exit fee" if I sell within a period of
  years?
- What is the 12 B-1 fee, and for how many years is it col-
  lected? Is it contingent on early withdrawal?
- Is it contingent on expense ratio?
- Is there a wrap charge (no commissions, but a fixed annual
  percentage covering expenses and broker's compensation)?

The issue of fees and commissions is so fraught with mathe-
matical calculations, predictions, and jargon that it's easy to persuade the investor for or against loads. For example, some of the
performance reports make loads look good because they don't take
out the fees and loads in calculating performance results. Other
reports tout no-loads no matter what, even if their performance is
poorer than a load fund.

So, here are my suggestions:

- Avoid funds with dividend reinvestment loads. They slow
  you down too much in making up for lost time.
- If you need a financial planner to get you on the path to
  making up for lost time, compensate him by following his
  load fund suggestions, as long as the performance of the funds
  is outstanding.

- If you buy a front-end load fund, plan to hold on to it. The longer you keep it, the more your up-front costs are amortized.
- If you plan to go in and out of funds, select no-loads.
- If you can select funds on your own, go with no-loads.
- Never forget the "Blue Suit Theory of Investing"—don't be stymied by a desire for perfection. In the end, you'll probably have some loads, some no-loads, and some duds—better than never having had mutual funds at all!

UNDERSTAND THE TAX CONSEQUENCES

Mutual funds are best kept in a tax-deferred plan. But even so, taxes must be paid someday. All income dividends and capital gains are taxable unless generated by Tier-One municipal bond funds. The change from one family of funds to another is a sale and can result in a gain or loss. *IRS Publication 564*, available free from the IRS, will tell you all the tax aspects of mutual fund ownership. Call 800-829-3676.

ONCE YOU HAVE SELECTED A FUND, KEEP UP WITH ITS PERFORMANCE

Read your mutual fund statement and follow the fund in *The Wall Street Journal*. Keep up as well with the financial press that rates funds. *Money, Forbes, Newsweek, and Worth*, all publish articles on funds regularly, and the Lipper Analytic Services compares funds quarterly. Ratings also can be obtained from the funds themselves and from financial professionals. Another tool for comparison is to review your fund's annual performance and that of the market as a whole in market index reports such as the Dow Jones Average, Standard & Poor's 500, the Dow Jones Industrial Average, or the Wilshire 5000 Equity Index.

The Wilshire is my favorite because it weighs the dollar value of all stocks listed on the NYSE and the AMEX, plus most over-the-counter stocks (stocks bought through brokers but not traded on an exchange). It is the most representative average and the best to judge your equity mutual fund.

To make this comparison, you will need to know how well your fund actually did. Each year you own your fund, ask the company or your financial professional for the annual percentage return. This percentage takes into account dividends, interest, and any other distributions, plus the change in value of a share in the mutual fund from the beginning of the year to the end.

To make interim checkups on changes in the NAV of your fund, you can look in *The Wall Street Journal* daily, if you like. First you will see the bid price (the sum you get when you sell) then the asked price (the price you pay when you buy). The difference between these is the load. The last column shows the change in NAV from the day before. Every time you get a distribution, add it to the change in NAV from the time you checked at the beginning of the year. At year's end you will know the total dollars your fund made or lost. Express this as a percentage of the initial investment and you will know your annual return.

THE BEST TIME TO BUY TIER-TWO MUTUAL FUNDS IS NOW

Making up for lost time requires immediate and disciplined action. Buy your funds now. I've been giving financial seminars for years and at every one there is a participant who asks, "Wouldn't it be better to wait until the market changes, the interest rates change, the election is over, the Messiah comes?" There is always a reason to delay. Don't buy into the two following wrong thoughts that are sure to do you in.

WRONG THOUGHT 1: IF I HAVE ONLY A LITTLE MONEY TO INVEST, I CAN NEVER MAKE UP FOR LOST TIME

The power of compound investing (reinvesting the return on your money) is so great that even small sums invested regularly pile up high. For example, $2,000 a year invested in an individual retirement account (IRA) adds up to $65,053 when you are six months away from age sixty (the age at which you can withdraw the funds without an IRS penalty) if you make your contributions starting at age forty.

Moreover, disciplined saving beats a onetime investment of a large sum. Investor A has $10,000 in a lump sum to invest; Investor B has $2,000 at the beginning of each year. After five years they both have invested the same amount of money (let's assume at 10 percent). While it is true that Investor A has more regardless of the investment rate of return, there is only a $4,000 difference on average.

But look what happens after the fifth year. Investor B continues with the $2,000-a-year contribution. He soon exceeds the amount initially invested by A. With the help of compounding, at the end of twenty years Investor B has accumulated $102,320 for his painless $40,000 of investing (assuming 10 percent interest).

Moral of the story: No matter how little you can invest, do it now.

WRONG THOUGHT 2: IF I HAVE A LUMP SUM TO INVEST, I AM BETTER OFF LEAVING IT IN A MONEY MARKET FUND AND SLOWLY INVESTING IT RATHER THAN MAKING A LUMP-SUM INVESTMENT NOW

The periodic investment of dollars into a mutual fund or other investment venture has long proved a good move for increasing your return. It works best when the period of investing is over ten years or more and all gains are reinvested. It is a nice, passive way to invest periodically over time.

For this reason, many people with a lump sum of money want to dribble it out as a market management measure. For those seeking to make up for lost time, this is not a good idea.

The time value of compound investing works best if you can maximize your initial investment. For example, Investor A, investing a lump sum of $10,000, has $56,044 at 9 percent after twenty years. Investor B has $91,523, but he invested $40,000 over that period of time. Investor A made more than five times his total investment, while Investor B made only a little more than two times his total investment.

As the years go by, this difference becomes greater. Especially if you are on the lighter side of forty, make an effort to sock away as much as you can immediately. Contribute big savings as early as possible in your making-up-for-lost-time strategy plan. Give your nonperforming assets a wake-up call. Get cash for jewelry you don't want, liquidate furniture and collections if your taste has outgrown them. Postpone the luxury purchase until next year and save today.

Choosing the Best

Tier-Three Investments

to Make Up for Lost Time

If you can't stand the heat, get out of the kitchen.

HARRY S TRUMAN

Tier-Three investments come in three categories:

- Tangibles—art, antiques, jewelry. The showy stuff also provides the psychological benefits of well-being.
- Commodities—gold, silver, metals, sugar, coffee, oil, etc. These are fast-moving, win-or-lose investments that are bought with a lot of leverage.
- Strategies—futures, options, warrants, selling short, buying on margin, etc. These are not really investments so much as investment strategies.

All of these investments fall into two very different groups: those, like arts and antiques, that give you an extraordinary boost because you have the know-how to buy right; and those, like options and futures, that give you an extraordinary boost because they can be highly leveraged (you control a large portfolio with a small amount of cash).

It is the latter that this chapter will describe. No matter which group you go with, however, *each takes a lot of work and is a special endeavor unto itself. You cannot be a dilettante investor when it comes to Tier Threes. In any category.* Whatever Tier-Three investment attracts you, remember these rules.

Six Essential Rules for Tier-Three Investing

1. *Be informed.* Become an expert and use your expertise to stay with one type of Tier Three. Don't spread yourself thin.

2. *Look for the investment, don't let it come looking for you.* Don't buy because a broker suggests it. You seek out the investment and the broker you will use. Don't let anyone rush you into buying.

3. *Go for the long haul.* Start small so that if you lose, you can keep trying.

4. *Know exactly the maximum you can lose and be sure you can afford to risk it.*

5. *Follow the eighteen-month rule.* Study the field for eighteen months before you invest. Do your investing on paper. Then, when your strategies have been working out, take the plunge.

6. *Invest only in Tier-Threes that you fully understand.*

Remember, Tier Threes are speculations, not investments. The difference is predictability. Tier Ones and Tier Twos, if held over time, have a reviewable history of performance. The performance history of a Tier-Three investment is much less of a measure of its future potential. You cannot rely on past performance as an indicator of future performance. Modern computer technologies are creating improved ways to reduce risk, as are mutual fund structures that diversify Tier-Three investments for the little guy. Meanwhile, use only money you can afford to lose.

The following is a synopsis of a variety of Tier-Three investments. Just to get you thinking, I have defined them, given you a few words of wisdom, some warnings, and (in the Bibliography) a few books to read. Bought wrong, Tier-Three investments can ruin lives. Bought right, they can make up for a lot of lost time, so it would be limiting of me if I left them out. It would be irresponsible of me, however, to claim that what follows is a definitive and complete Tier-Three investment guide.

REAL ESTATE

One type of Tier-Three investment is real estate (not your residence). This is so important as a potential money-maker that I have devoted two entire chapters to it (Chapters 22 and 23).

ART, ANTIQUES, AND COLLECTIBLES

Officially, an antique is anything over one hundred years old, and art is in the eye of the beholder. As a Tier-Three investment, art, antiques, and collectibles must be items that have a ready market, through stores or galleries; through auctions; through advertising in art, antiques, and collectibles magazines; or through organized art, collectible, and antique shows.

Words of wisdom: Don't confuse these tangibles with your furniture. Money is made here by actively buying and selling these items. Everyone will tell you not to buy art or antiques unless you love them. Wrong. If you love it, you won't sell it; and that's not investing. Don't buy what you love, buy what interests you, whether it's old lace or Dutch masters. Research the market, haunt auction houses, sell on a regular basis, and use the profit to trade up for better quality in the same category. By the time you are ready to retire, you may have a fine painting, an impressive collection of stamps, or a museum-quality rug. Sell whatever you have and invest the proceeds for income from a Tier-One investment.

Better yet, give your tangibles to a charitable trust, have it sell them and invest the proceeds for you free of capital-gains tax. Receive the income for life and give the trust the principal when you die. The gift will also give you a handy income tax deduction that will allow you to invest your post-retirement dollars in higher-interest-paying taxable investments like Treasuries rather than in lower-paying tax-frees like municipal bonds.

Warning: Don't buy fads and forecasts. My eleven-year-old son tries to persuade me to eat at McDonalds because he says the toys you get will be a collectible. He could be right, but they're still not an investment.

THE COLLATERAL CONCEPT AND TIER THREES

A positive feature of an investment is how well it serves as collateral (security pledged to a creditor) and how easily it can be leveraged. A wealthy young couple once came to me for help in getting a mortgage. They had a net worth of over $3,000,000 but it was all in paintings. A regular bank was reluctant to use art as collateral. Eventually I advised them to become the private banking clients of a large international bank, and as a courtesy for their business they got their mortgage.

Some investments, most notably real estate, can be highly leveraged. This means that you can put some money down and go into debt for the rest. All the security you need is the new real estate itself. The purchase creates its own collateral. Other investments like annuities and mutual funds require you to pay 100 percent cash. Once you own them, however, they become collateral, so you can borrow money from a bank to get cash if you need it.

If you want to take the risk, you can also use your Tier-One and Tier-Two investments as collateral, calculated by trading in a margin account. A margin account is an account opened with your stockbroker and some banks so you can buy stock with less than 100 percent cash. If an investor believes in the growth of a stock and wishes to purchase more than he or she can afford, an investor can do so "on margin." The Federal Reserve System sets the minimum amount of cash that must be placed in a margin account. The minimum is expressed in terms of a percentage of the market value of the portfolio. If the market value goes down, the cash is insufficient and the investor must come up with more. This is a "margin call."

For example, if your account requires a margin of 50 percent, you need pay only one half the actual price of the stocks you wish to purchase. But the cash plus the value of the portfolio in your account must always be equal to one half the cost of your original purchase. If the stocks go up, you have additional credit to buy more stocks (up to double the amount of the value of the portfolio minus what you already used up to make purchases). If the stock goes down, you have insufficient collateral against your debt, and you will receive a margin maintenance call.

Once you have set up a margin account, the individual brokerage house or bank determines how much cash is necessary to maintain the margin. Some require no more than 30 percent of the original purchase price as collateral. For investors picking and trading individual stocks, the margin account is an important tool. But for others trying to make up for lost time, it is a siren's song that can deplete the value of Tier-Two investing by making speculation too easy. If you decide to use margin accounts, beware of the interest rates you are charged, and make sure that the deal is better than other forms of borrowing. Remember also that if you can't make good on your margin call, your broker or banker will become a creditor like any other.

LEVERAGE AND SPECULATION

The heart of Tier-Three speed money-making is the use of leverage with fast-paced investing strategies. For example, today $1,000 will buy an option to purchase 5,000 ounces of silver. (Options always consist of 5,000 ounces of silver. But depending on the market, an option may be purchased for as little as $50 to over $2,000.) If you bought the silver itself instead of an option to purchase silver, you would pay: 5,000 ounces × $4.30/ounce = $21,500. Leverage operates in a slightly different way in each type of Tier Three. Let's see how it works:

FUTURES

A commodity is a blanket term for tangibles like metals (gold, platinum, silver), agribiz products (pork bellies, sugar, coffee, wheat), and petroleum products (light and crude oil).

A future is a contract to buy a certain commodity at a certain price on a certain date, i.e., you agree to pay a specific price for pork bellies on a certain date in March. However, you need only place 10 to 20 percent down on the contract. The speculation is that pork bellies will rise in price by then and you will sell your contract to someone who actually wants to take possession of pork bellies in March (i.e., a bacon producer) or another speculator who believes they will go higher before the contract expires. Sometimes the price will rise minutes after you purchased the future, so you sell at a fast profit. Sometimes the price never rises. In March, those pork bellies are yours unless you sell at a loss to another person.

Go to your video store and rent *Trading Places*, starring Eddie Murphy and Dan Aykroyd, to learn how fast the commodities market moves and how it is driven by weather, politics, fruit flies, and OPEC prices. Then rent Barbra Streisand's *For Pete's Sake*, and see what happens when you must take delivery of the pork bellies.

Many speculators are willing to take the risk of futures trading, but they can't afford it. Although you need only put up 10 to 20 percent of the contract price when you buy (leverage), you must come up with the full contract price if you don't sell. Only 3 percent of all futures speculation results in delivery. You can also instruct your broker to sell at a loss with a stop-loss order. This requires your broker to sell at a specified price in order to keep your loss at a certain level. But, you must move quickly to sell your contract and limit your loss before it expires.

MANAGED FUTURES ACCOUNTS

Managed futures accounts are accounts opened with a commodities trading adviser (CTA), a specialist in the field of commodities trading. A managed futures account is just like a brokerage account in structure, but the items purchased are limited to commodities contracts. The CTA is compensated (very well) by a fee based on the amount under management and on the performance of the account. CTAs often earn 20 percent of what they earn for you. The key to success here is not you, but the performance of the CTA. He or she makes all the decisions, including when not to invest. CTAs are rated by past performance. A managed futures account can diversify and enrich an already substantial portfolio, but it must not be used as a desperate attempt to make up for lost time overnight.

Words of wisdom: Visit your CTA before you hire him or her, even if the office is in another state. Read the disclosure documents, get references, obtain an account of the CTA's past performance. Ask about the CTA's investing philosophy and how the CTA actually makes decisions. Is your money always in play? Does the CTA use a computer system to make decisions? Try to understand the system.

Warning: You are giving up control of your money to someone who will virtually be gambling with it. The industry is self-regulated by the National Futures Association and government-regulated by the Commodities Futures Trading Commission. Don't get the two confused and don't confuse their literature. The former is a trade association and the latter a government agency. If you decide to take the plunge, be prepared for fast losses and possibly fast gains. And speaking of fast losses and gains, enter the option.

Warning: The attraction of speculating in futures is the leverage. It is also the downside. If prices move against you by the amount of your margin, you can be *more* than wiped out. You can owe more than your initial investment plus brokerage fees, especially if you don't move fast enough to sell and limit your loss.

OPTIONS ON FUTURES

An option is the right to buy something in the future at a price agreed to by contract in the present. The right to buy at that price does not last forever; options have an expiration date. If the date passes without the option being exercised or sold, the option cost is forfeited. Options are called a wasting asset, since as the expiration date draws closer, the value of the option declines.

There are several types of options. One is an option on commodities futures. For example, if you think the value of pork bellies will go up, you pay for the right to buy a futures contract at a specified price, as long as you exercise the option by a certain date. If the price goes up, you exercise the option and sell the contract at the higher price. You pocket the difference. If prices stay low, you probably must let the option expire and lose the money you paid for it.

Note: certain other factors do apply. An investor's risk when buying options is limited to the premium, commission, and applicable fees. Most commodity options require a $5,000 buy-in; that's the limit of your loss.

You can also sell options. If you already own a contract, you can sell the right to buy at a certain price. If the prices stay low, you pocket the amount paid to you for the option. If prices rise, you must sell the contract at the low option price and lose the benefit of the high prices.

STOCK OPTION TRADING

Another type of option trading is with stocks. This involves owning shares of stock and selling the option of the stock being bought from you at a specific price, on a specific date called the expiration date. For example, you own a hundred shares of AT&T stock with a market value of $100 per share. You don't think the price will rise, but someone else does. He pays you $300 for the right to buy the stock from you at $120 per share within the next three months. That $300 is called a premium (and is taxable income to you whether or not the option is exercised).

If the price never reaches $120 or more, you keep the $300. The option expires and you keep the stock. If the stock rises above the option price, the buyer can call the stock (exercise the option) at $120 per share. You still keep the $300 and the $120 per share. You have made $20 per share. If the stock is then worth $150, the buyer will make the $30-per-share profit. This kind of option selling is called "selling covered calls." It is a conservative form of Tier-Three investing and can provide some extra income if you own stocks. It can be an enhancement to Tier-Two investing.

The option purchaser is the one who may make big money because he is controlling the ownership of the hundred shares of stock without buying it. If the option expires, only its cost is lost. In this example, the buyer would lose the $300 he paid to you if he chose to let the option expire. If you are a Tier-Two investor with knowledge of individual stocks, you may want to use stock option buying as your Tier-Three speculation.

Warning: There are commissions with every purchase and sale of a stock or option. Take costs and taxes into consideration before you get stars in your eyes. A very dangerous game is selling "uncovered calls." In an uncovered call, you don't buy any stock, but you sell the option to buy a stock at a specific price. You bet that the option will expire and that you will pocket the premium. If the option is exercised, you must go out and buy the stock at a higher price than the option contract. You'd better have the money to make good on the call.

You can also "sell a put," so called because it permits the buyer to put stock to you (force you to buy stock) at a given price. Once again, you own no stock, but you believe that a particular stock will go up. You sell your willingness to buy it at a specified price. A person who owns the stock believes that the price may go down, but isn't sure that it will. To protect himself he buys your put, so he can get the put price from you.

For example, Ms. A owns a hundred shares of AT&T stock presently worth $100 per share. She thinks it might go down but doesn't want to sell. For a premium of $300 paid immediately, you sell her the right to sell the shares to you any time in the next three months for $90. If prices go up, she doesn't sell and you keep the premium. If prices dip below $90, you must buy at $90 and she has minimized her loss.

CLOSED-END FUNDS

A less volatile form of Tier-Three investing with stocks involves closed-end mutual funds. Closed-end funds are mutual funds that issue a fixed number of shares. They cannot grow by increasing the number of investment shares. The shares are sold on the stock exchanges through a broker. Closed-end funds usually are sold at a discount per share below their net asset value. For example, if the total market value of the assets held, divided by the number of outstanding shares, would give you $20 per share, the actual sales price per share might be $18. It's much like buying an undervalued stock: Buy at a discount and sell when the discount is less, then take your profit.

If you plan to buy and hold a closed-end fund because you like its performance over time, you are making a Tier-Two growth investment. It is the buy-at-discount and sell-when-the-discount-is-less strategy that is a Tier-Three speed-investing technique.

If you believe in the economic growth of a foreign country like Spain or Germany, you can invest in its future with a closed-end country fund. These buys can be made only through a broker. Closed-end funds are listed and rated in the same mutual fund books recommended in Chapter 9.

To make the best use of a closed-end fund, you must develop a strategy.

Make a list of several funds using the mutual fund materials suggested in Chapter 9.

Scan back issues of the financial newspapers to track past increases and decreases in discounts.

Find a broker who will be able to provide a report of how the fund rose and fell over several years.

Make a mental "sell order," that is, decide how much the discount must go down in order for you to sell.

Keep your promise to yourself to sell at that time. Take your profit and start again.

Unlike art and some real estate, the closed-end fund can be bought in a pension plan, and taxes on gains can be deferred.

Warning: Don't buy brand-new funds. They have no track record and commissions are high.

SELLING SHORT

Another way of using leverage with stock investments is called "selling short." If you believe that a stock will decline in value, you can sell it today and buy it at a lower price tomorrow. In this way you make a profit before ever owning the stock! However, you must buy and transfer the shares you sell (but don't yet own) by the fifth day after a trade.

You perform this trick by borrowing the shares from your broker and delivering the brokerage house's shares on the due date. Within a period of five days' time you replace or "cover" this borrowing. If the price does decline, you make a nice profit. If the price rises, you take a loss. If you can't afford to cover, you have a debt.

HOW TO IMPROVE YOUR CHANCES AT MAKING UP FOR LOST TIME WITH TIER THREES

Many commentators state that as much as 85 percent of all commodity speculators lose money, and that financial futures speculation is successful only 20 percent of the time. Further, once you bring investment debt or high leverage into the picture with any kind of investment, you have turned a Tier-One or Tier-Two investment into a speculation: a Tier-Three investment. Many conservative investments, like blue-chip stocks and income-producing real estate, become very risky when leveraged. Don't be fooled by the nature of the underlying investment. Safety is not only in what you buy, but in the debt risk you take to buy it.

Even so, no book on making up for lost time is complete without guidelines for your becoming part of the winning minority who use leverage and speculation to make large profits fast. To improve the odds of success, whether in commodities, options, or futures, there are certain things you must do.

If You Are Interested in Buying Stock Options

- Start with a $10,000 pot. Study ten to twenty corporations on whose stock options are traded. Follow your picks for three months without investing. Remember that commissions eat up a portion of profits, so take them into consideration.

   Remember that profits from options are short-term and taxed at your top rate. When you calculate how well you did during your three-month dry run, take into account both commissions and taxes.

- To maximize the effects of leverage, buy long-term options on stocks that are "out of the money" (not near the strike price, which is the price at which you may exercise your option). These are the least expensive options to buy, providing you with the most leverage. In a bull market (where stock prices are rising), you will control a lot of shares, and it's to be hoped that some options will be exercised at a profit.

   In a super bull market, you can buy options closer to the expiration date as long as the strike price is pretty close to the market price at the time you buy the option. If the stock increases in value, exercise your option and take your profit. If the option expires before you exercise, your loss is limited to the option price.

As you become more sophisticated in buying and selling puts and calls, you may decide to enter into option strategies. Spreads, straddles, strips, and straps are all names for combinations of buying and selling puts and calls at different strike prices and exercise dates, on the same or different stocks.

To make up for lost time using these strategies, it is absolutely essential that you become an expert and stick to your last. If you get the hang of a strategy, stay with it. Expand slowly. Most important, when you make a profit, put part of it away in a growth mutual fund (Tier Two). Use the rest to reinvest in Tier-Three option trading.

If You Are Interested in Financial Futures and Indexes

Financial futures trading is like trading in commodities futures except that the "commodity" is financial paper like Treasury bills, certificates of deposit, and collateralized mortgage obligations. In other words, you are "betting" on the fate of interest rates on Tier-One investments. If you think you can predict the rise and fall in interest rates, you may have an opportunity to make up for lost time with buying and selling options on financial futures. Options to buy cost roughly $100 each, and strategies parallel those of buying stock options.

Speculating in financial futures began as a hedge (protection) for institutional investors with millions in Tier-One investments. If the market value of their Tier Ones declined, a successful investment in financial futures would make the balance sheet look better. Very wealthy individual investors also often use financial futures trading to protect their Tier-One holdings (this is called hedging).

If your forte is predicting the stock market (Tier Two) instead of the debt market (Tier One), you can speculate in stock indexes. These are like buying commodities contracts, only stocks are substituted for pork bellies.

Stock indexes are composite valuations of a number of stocks (Standard & Poor's 500, Standard & Poor's 100, Value Line Futures, and others). These indexes are tools for judging the direction of the overall stock market. They have now become speculations in themselves. You can buy puts and calls on these indexes and control more than $75,000 of stock value with an investment of approximately $300.

Option strategies on financial futures and indexes again parallel those for commodities and individual stocks.

IF YOU ARE INTERESTED IN GOLD

Investing in gold, in and of itself, is not a Tier-Three speed investment. On the contrary, buying bullion, gold certificates, or shares in mining companies are all ways to protect your buying power in the event of high inflation.

Buying gold to make up for lost time is a failure in noninflationary times. After retirement, however, when the buying power of your money replaces the earning power of your labor, gold becomes an important inflation-fighting strategy.

By contrast, gold futures and options on gold futures are Tier-Three speed investments. Many small investors understand metals more easily than agricultural products; for them, commodities trading in metals could be the road to take. Gold futures can be handled by most brokers and are actively traded on the COMEX and LMX (London Metal Exchange). Leverage is a plus. You need only put down from 5 to 15 percent of the price of gold futures contracts, which are sold in 100-ounce lots. Money can be made quickly with little cash outlay.

As with other commodities, to limit your exposure, you can trade gold options. The system for doing this is identical to the options procedure (see page 97). Spreads and other strategies are also available in buying gold futures and options.

IF YOU ARE INTERESTED IN PEACE OF MIND AND SMELLING THE ROSES

In the college courses on finance that I taught, I gave my students an end-of-year blessing: "May you marry commodities traders because they are very rich and they are never home!"

That, to tell the truth, is about the long and the short of it. A dabbler in any of these speculations will likely lose money, but those capable of keeping a sustained interest, working hard, studying, taking chances, losing at first and staying in the game can get rich. Is it worth it, when simply dollar cost averaging will get you pretty close to a realistic, comfortable future? As comedian Jackie Mason would say, "It's up to you."

PART III

ow to Make the Right Investment

Choice Every Time!

Using Investment Pace to
Make Up for Lost Time

It's the story of the tortoise and the hare. Now, this little story
isn't fair. 'Cause the bunny kept a-runnin', and the tortoise was
slow comin'. Yet the winner was the tortoise, not the hare.

ADRIANE G. BERG,
Your Wealth-Building Years

Investment pace is the expected gain from an investment over the
length of time you have in which to invest. Pace and risk are usually
directly proportionate to each other. The faster the reward, the
higher the risk, so you want to use a fast-paced investment only if
it's worth the risk.

For example, historically, common stocks have been the highest
appreciating assets. Over the years, the added risk of common stocks
over bonds really paid off. One thousand dollars invested in the
average government bond over the last half century would be worth
approximately $20,000 today. The same investment in stocks di-
versified to a whopping $650,000.

To make a wise allocation among the Three Tiers, you must
have a grasp of the pace and risk you can expect in each tier.
Then you can allocate your assets by selecting the lowest-risk investment that will perform at the pace you require to make up for
lost time.

A LOOK AT HISTORICAL PACE

The Ibbotson Association, an independent research group in Chicago, did a well-respected study on past performance of major investments from 1926 to 1991:

	50 Years	25 Years	10 Years	5 Years
Small-Company Stocks	16.3%	12.4%	11.6%	13.6%
Large-Company Stocks	12.6	10.6	16.2	15.9
Long-Term Corpo-rate Bonds	5.4	8.8	13.1	12.5
Intermediate-Term U.S. Govern-ment Bonds	5.6	9.0	11.0	10.3
Treasury Bills	4.6	7.2	6.9	6.3

SOURCE: Adapted From T. Rowe Price's *Asset Allocation* brochure, 1993.

From this data you can see that large-company stocks have a history of yielding a compound annual percent return of 12.6 percent (compound annual percent return is calculated by assuming that the money earned as a result of the stock's rate of return is immediately reinvested and also earns the same return).

Small-company stocks over the same period did better, earning 16.3 percent. Treasury bills did the worst at 4.6 percent, and long-term corporate bonds were an improvement over government bonds. Intermediate-term bonds (five to seven years until the maturity date) earned more than long-term bonds (up to thirty years until the maturity date).

This means that if you had invested in a diversified portfolio of small emerging growth companies in 1926, you would have the most money possible from your investments by 1992. Although we do not have fifty years of investing time, it is still my belief that with ten or more years before retirement, we are best off with a diversified portfolio largely composed of Tier-Two investments with sprinklings of Tier-One and Tier-Three investments.

WHY YOU NEED ALL THREE TIERS TO MAKE UP FOR LOST TIME

It is wishful thinking to conclude that mutual funds alone invested in equities is all the allocation you will need. For one thing, if you have a very short time in which to make up for lost time, you cannot rely on the performance history of stocks over long periods. For another, there is the risk factor to consider. As you get closer to retirement, you cannot take the chance of working out of a bad market. So you naturally will shift your portfolio from Tier Two into Tier One.

So, to help you set up your portfolio, here are my "frognostications" (jumping to conclusions) for the next twenty years:

Tier-One bonds and other Tier Ones—6.8 to 8.2 percent

Tier-Two common stocks and/or index funds—13.4 percent

Diversified Tier-Two mutual funds and non-blue-chip common stocks—14.1 percent

Inflation—5.5 percent

BASIC MAKING-UP-FOR-LOST-TIME (MUFLT) PORTFOLIO

Let's take a look at a hypothetical investor. This investor is twenty years away from retirement, needs a total return of 12 percent to meet her goal, and is of average-risk tolerance. She has

20 percent in small cap companies

25 percent in maximum- or aggressive-growth companies

20 percent in international equities

20 percent in a mixture of the agriculture and/or pharmaceutical sector

5 percent in gold bullion

10 percent in a well-managed futures or other speculative account

Assuming she allocates her assets among mutual funds, she might choose

Montgomery Small Cap

Kaufmann Fund

Govett International

Oppenheimer Global Bio-Tech

Bullion purchased from a dealer

Managed futures account run by a CTA

A closed-end fund such as the First Philippine Fund

All these funds show a regular total return of 12 percent or better, many of them substantially better. The closed-end fund and futures account are speculations. But this investor has chosen products that should exceed her goal needs over time, so there is room to take a few chances.

As she gets closer to retirement, this allocation of investments gets too risky. They haven't changed; she has. If there is a temporary dive in value, she has less time to wait it out. She will need to recalculate the miminum total return she needs. If all went well in previous MUFLT years, she may need to earn no more on her portfolio than will keep up with inflation. If so, she can switch into guaranteed investments like government bonds and bank instruments.

In short, this MUFLT portfolio is not a model portfolio. It is a *paced portfolio*. The investor chooses investments with a track record of total return that is equal to or slightly better than the investment return required to meet her goal. If the risk is too high, the investor changes her pace and/or adjusts her goal. If the investor is close to reaching her goal, she can pace for safety or exceed the goal.

At what pace must your investments grow to meet your goal? Once you know, you can select the right investment based on its past "pace" history. You can choose among the many equally paced investments based on their cost, risk, convenience, and simplicity.

To accomplish all this, it is necessary to state your goals and calculate your needs. You'll do this in the next chapter.

FINANCIAL VIRTUAL REALITY:

FACING YOUR RETIREMENT GAP

Sometimes I think I would like to go live in a cabin in the woods.

No tax insurance, alimony, repairs.

> ANNE TYLER,
> *Searching for Caleb*

Most baby boomers have a 40 percent retirement gap. They will retire at 60 percent of their wished-for assets. This is caused by a combination of great expectations and lack of planning. For many, the lack of planning stems from associating retirement with hard-to-face old age. But retirement is a goal, not a punishment. It is the freedom to live job-free forever even if you choose to work anyway.

To meet your retirement goal, these three steps are musts.

STEP 1: MAKE PERSONAL ASSUMPTIONS

Choose your retirement age.

Count the number of years until retirement.

Figure out inflation rate (use 4 percent as a rule of thumb).

Decide the total income you need at retirement and during the
    years in retirement—a nice way of focusing on mortality—
    use your insurance company's guidelines and a knowledge of
    your genetics.

Focus on a retirement date. If you can't decide on a date, do the calculations in this part for every five years from age fifty-five to seventy.

Arrive at a "retirement salary." You can create a few budgets and use each one in your calculations, or you can simply take 80 percent of your present expenditures to reach a ballpark figure. The closer you are to retirement, the easier your target goal will be to define, and the more important precision planning is as well.

Calculate how much of your money will be available to meet the goal. Most of you will obtain your retirement income from a combination of these five sources: pensions at work, social security, sale of your house, personal savings, and insurance plans and annuities. You will have to contact your pension group, insurance agent, and Social Security office to learn the income you can expect.

STEP 2: STARE THE NUMBERS IN THE FACE

Calculate your retirement gap (the difference between your goal income at retirement and your actual available income). Use the following formula—it's as simple as I could make it:

1. Annual post-retirement income for you and your mate after taxes. Include social security, pension income, trust funds, royalties, etc.

2. Annual expenditures at retirement. Create a detailed budget or take 80 percent of your present expenditures (page 51).

3. Annual income from your independent savings. Take your net worth from page 49, and use the chart on page 61 to determine your savings growth by time of retirement. Then use the chart on page 60 to determine the annual income you will derive.

4. Add lines 1 and 3. Subtract that number from line 2. This is your annual retirement income shortfall.

For greatest accuracy, be sure to take taxes into consideration. The taxation of social security, pensions, and other income will be discussed throughout this book. You can also integrate inflation into these numbers with the use of the software listed in the Bibliography, the help of your financial planner, or by contacting T. Rowe Price, a mutual fund company, for its *Retirement Planning Workbook*, available free at this time by calling 1-800-225-5132.

If you have no income gap, you can put down this book and retire now. You are still reading? Then let's go on to the next step.

STEP 3: WORK WITH THE NUMBERS

Calculate the lump sum you must accumulate by retirement in order to make up for the shortfall. Use the chart on page 60 to determine the amount you will need in order to generate the shortfall of income at the rate you assume you will be able to earn on your money at retirement. This is the lump sum for which you must save. Now, look at the chart of page 58 to see how much you must save each year to meet your goal.

Here's a quick way to calculate this that doesn't require you to turn any pages. Assume that your savings will double in eight years. These are the factors by which you must divide the lump sum you need at retirement in order to determine how much of it you must save each year to meet your goal:

Number of Years Until Retirement	*Factor*
10	17.5
15	35.3
20	63.3
25	107.0
30	174.0

If this yearly "nut" seems too impossible to crack, there are several things you can do. First, see if you are being too conservative. Increase the total return and recalculate the power of your savings at a higher rate.

Second, change your retirement income requirements and your nest egg goal by downscaling.

Third, liquidate and spend your principal after retirement. Multiply the number of years in retirement (see the chart below) by the income you want each year. What figure did you get? If this nest egg gives you a lower "nut," you can save less. Just take this figure and find it on the chart on page 58, and see how much you must save each year to accumulate the amount.

Present Age	Years in Retirement	
	Individual	*Couple*
55	28	34
60	24	30
65	20	25
70	16	21
75	12	16

Fourth, work for more years and add to savings.

You can change these assumptions several times to get different pictures of your future. Plug different assumptions into the calculations until you get the unique combination that works best for you.

RETIREMENT PLANNING FOR A GENERATION OF MATH PHOBICS

If you have followed the calculations so far, you have a clearer picture of your retirement goals than do 90 percent of your peers. But that's not good enough. You have had to estimate the rate of inflation, the annual growth or interest on your savings, your tax bracket (before and after retirement), even how long you will live.

Precision planning is hard without help. In the Bibliography you will find out how to order computer software that will do many of the calculations for you. Or, you may prefer to work with a financial planner and "let George do it." See Chapter 15 for advice in choosing a professional.

Your Model Three-Tier

Portfolio

Increasingly, the mathematics will demand courage to face its implications.

MICHAEL CRICHTON,
Jurassic Park

There are many roads to monetary success. To help you, a financial plan must fit your special needs. That's why I don't believe in one overall program generically good for all. Still, I sympathize with the need for guidelines, and so does the financial-planning and investment industry. For the past three years, two new concepts have been developed for the purpose of simplifying your life, helping you get on with the task of investing, and, of course, helping the industry make sales. These concepts are (1) asset allocation and (2) model portfolio design.

ASSET ALLOCATION FOR THOSE WHO WANT TO MAKE UP FOR LOST TIME

Asset allocation is an umbrella term that describes a number of different systems used to determine what percentage of your money should go into each of the Three Tiers at any given time. It's like taking all of your money and dealing it out in piles of growth,

income, and speculation. Assets are allocated in terms of percent-
ages in each tier. Depending on several factors such as risk tolerance,
number of years to retirement, and your health, you may get a
slightly different allocation. Nevertheless, allocation exemplifies
two overriding principles that we already understand from several
discussions in this book:

1. DIVERSIFICATION OF ASSETS: OWNING MORE
   THAN ONE TYPE OF ASSET DECREASES YOUR
   RISK OF LOSS. IF THE MARKET IN ONE OF THE
   TIERS FALLS, THE ASSETS IN THE OTHER
   TIERS OFTEN STAY THE SAME OR INCREASE.

This is not a difficult concept, but most people do not implement
the idea of diversification. They understand it, but they just don't
do it. For example, many baby boomers are 80 percent or more in
real estate. Many older people are up to 100 percent in Tier-One
lending investments.

In Chapter 1 you focused on why you have the investments you
have today. The answer to that is your clue at how adept you will
be in asset allocation. If you are heavily in one tier, it may be fear
of change, an adviser who leads you to one type of investment,
habit, lack of knowledge, or reluctance to spend time on personal
finance.

Most of you will relate to one or more of those reasons. If you
feel that you cannot, or do not, wish to overcome your reluctance
to diversify, find a financial planner (Chapter 15) to do it for you.
Or, you may want to use the software packages found in the
Bibliography.

But What About Andrew Mellon?

The legendary financier and robber baron Andrew Mellon said,
"Put all your eggs in one basket, and watch that basket." Wouldn't
it be best, then, to have a guru prepare the finest stock portfolio
or select the best piece of real estate and just watch your net worth
grow? Yes, in the world of Plato's utopia, where philosophers are

king and all is perfect, it would. But in modern economic markets, nothing stays perfect for long, and asset allocation creates a balance.

2. PURPOSE DICTATES ALLOCATION: ALLOCATIONS DIFFER DEPENDING ON THE GOAL OF THE INVESTOR.

Asset allocation systems are not based per se on what makes you the most money. To do that requires clairvoyance. Instead, the allocations between each tier depend on whether you want growth of capital, income for living, preservation of capital for heirs, immediate liquidity to buy a house, or cash flow to pay off debts.

You already are familiar with each of the Three Tiers of investing and know generally the purposes they each fulfill, but when it comes to actually investing money, you must be more specific. Enter the model portfolio.

PRETTY AS A PICTURE

A model portfolio is a picture of the asset allocation you should make, together with the details of the investment within each tier that you should select. Remember that it is my view that the specifics are less critical to your wealth and well-being than the general allocation (see the "Blue Suit Theory of Investing," page 33).

Model portfolios match your goals with the proper asset allocation to meet them, by the target date of your choice. Obviously, no two people will have the same allocations, yet model portfolios found in most books and financial literature attempt to standardize investing by making assumptions regarding these factors and more. They then present pie charts showing the percentage of assets that you should have in each tier.

I prefer to use historical pace, common sense, and the "Blue Suit Theory of Investing" to choose investments. I hope you will use this chapter not to copy model portfolios, but to create a Sam portfolio, a Charlotte portfolio, a Julio portfolio, a Jamal portfolio, a Blackhawk portfolio, or one for whoever you are!

SCENARIO 1: STARTING FROM SCRATCH WITH WELL-PAYING JOBS

John and Joan are corporate executives with a combined salary of $150,000. They are forty years old and have never saved a dime. They plan to retire at age seventy on an income of $150,000 a year. They anticipate high inflation of 4.5 percent.

John has a defined benefit plan that was recently terminated by his firm. Joan has no pension at work. Their social security and the amount John will derive from the pension already vested will give the couple $50,000 in income.

To accumulate $1,000,000 worth of buying power in thirty years at 4.5 percent inflation they need a nest egg of $3,745,318. In order to do this, they must save $1,061 per month if they get 12 percent total return.

Given the historic pace of stocks, to make up for lost time they need only duplicate the performance of the stock market. Index funds like Vanguard Index Trust (1-800-851-4999) and SEI Index (1-800-342-5734) are just some of the funds that hold only those stocks used to make up the Standard & Poor's 500—in other words, the largest companies trading at any given time. Over the last five years most such funds have exceeded 12 percent.

Our couple can opt for such a "plain vanilla portfolio" because they have given themselves an extra five years to make up for lost time. What happens if they opt to retire at age sixty-eight instead?

Now, their portfolio must earn 12.5 percent in order to work for them. A slightly more aggressive move to a "quant"-style index fund can do it. These funds make their selection from among the five hundred following the S&P proportion of types of stocks, i.e., oil, industrial, retail; but they pick and choose the potential best performers from each group. Two quant funds are Laurel Stock (1-800-544-8888) and Vanguard Quantitative (1-800-851-4999).

SCENARIO 2: WAKING UP AT FIFTY AND
SHOOTING FOR A "NICE LIFE"

Rex and Alice are a typical making-up-for-lost-time couple. They have saved $30,000 in a money market fund. They have a total of $75,000 in self-directed IRAs and a KEOGH (Rex has his own business). And Alice just started a word-processing business after their last child went off to college.

They want to retire at age sixty-five with an annual retirement salary of $40,000. They assume a 4 percent inflation rate. To make up their shortfall, they need a lump sum at retirement of $431,333 in today's dollars if they earn 6 percent after retirement, and if they plan to spend-down their principal (these figures are adjusted for inflation). They can get this by investing $750 per month at 10 percent.

They can do this in one of three ways, depending on their risk tolerance.

RISK TOLERANCE

For a moderately high-risk portfolio they can invest

75 percent in stocks—25 percent in foreign stocks, 30 percent in small-company stocks, and 45 percent in large-company stocks (they can use index/quant)

20 percent in bonds—of which 10 percent can be foreign

  5 percent in money market funds

But let's say the couple is unsure of the viability of Rex's business and they might want to retire earlier. They can get about 95 percent of the result they need and reduce the potential for loss in the worst year to 60 percent of the moderately high-risk portfolio by rearranging the combination to

60 percent in stocks

20 percent in bonds

20 percent in cash

To reduce the risk of loss in any given year to 36 percent that of the first portfolio, the couple can realize only 88 percent of the gain by investing

50 percent in stocks

30 percent in bonds

20 percent in cash

This means that if this couple wants to keep a flexible retirement date, they can do so if they are willing to retire on the income from 12 percent fewer assets.

Again, the many choices here boil down to a few actual fund investments for this couple to consider:

Stocks

Corporate Leaders (1-800-544-8888)

Fidelity Advisor (1-800-522-7297)

Putnam Fund for Growth (1-800-225-1581)

Foreign Stocks

Harbor International (1-800-422-1050)

Templeton Foreign (1-800-237-0738)

T. Rowe Price International Fund (1-800-541-8832)

Bonds

Fidelity Balanced (1-800-544-8888)

USAA Mutual Income (1-800-531-8181)

Foreign Bonds

Merrill Lynch Global Bond B (1-800-333-9701 ext. 8836)

Scudder International Government (1-800-225-2470)

Van Eck World Income (1-800-221-2220)

Don't be curious about how I selected the funds. True to the "Blue Suit Theory of Investing," I didn't sweat it. I looked at a few magazines and books (listed in Chapter 9) for their rankings. I picked both loads and no-loads, based on overall costs and performance rankings.

I did, though, use three subtle points in selecting. For the foreign stock funds, I selected only those that invest abroad, not a combination of foreign and domestic. As for the growth stocks, I chose value-oriented funds instead of just good performers. At present the market is overvalued and I don't want the angst of a big correction next year. Value stocks are good performers without inflated prices. For the bonds, I selected "total return" funds that may have some stocks. This is more aggressive and works best for those making up for lost time. All of these fund categories are the traditional ones you will find in any financial journal describing funds.

If I were using an annuity, I would select from the same categories and in the same proportions. If I were selecting individual stocks and bonds, I would diversify in the same categories, but I would need a lot of money to do as good a job.

SCENARIO 3: FIVE YEARS UNTIL RETIREMENT AND REALLY SCARED

Paul and Paula are fifty-eight and sixty respectively. They have just emerged from a bankruptcy caused by severe real estate and business reversals. All of a sudden, this couple must rebuild from scratch. (This scenario is being played out nationwide by sudden widows, fired employees unable to find work for several months, those who have been ill, and some who just never saved for the future.)

Naturally, they must adjust retirement age and expectations. They also can resolve to spend the assets they finally accumulate. If they can earn 6 percent a year on their money (the average Tier-One return), they can spend the following percentage of their principal each year for the following number of years:

Percentage of Principal	Years It Will Last
6	49
7	28
8	21
9	17
10	14

But even the planner who resolves to reformulate retirement goals in the cold light of reality needs to start to save and invest money. This couple's portfolio is an odd combination of the very conservative and more aggressive.

First, they must build a solid base with a fund that asset-allocates their initial investments fast: T. Rowe Price Spectrum Funds for Growth (1-800-638-5660) accepts $2,500; Fidelity Asset Manager (1-800-544-8888) will start you with less.

As the couple saves additional dollars, they can invest them in these funds. Once they have acquired at least a $5,000 nest egg, the couple must make a fundamental making-up-for-lost-time decision: How big a chance do they want to take for the reward?

If the answer is very little, they can stay with this automatic diversification or soon become more sophisticated. They can earn 9 percent until retirement, when they would turn to traditional Tier-One bond funds for their 6 percent income stream.

If they are satisfied that they have enough to pay their basic expenses and are ready to take chances, the couple can instead invest new savings into mid- and small-cap funds. These are the most volatile and historically give the best returns—more than 20 percent in three years is not unheard of. Some examples are Kaufman Fund (1-800-237-0132), John Hancock Special Equities (1-800-225-5291), and Aim Constellation (1-800-347-4246). These funds are the most likely to charge loads. So, this couple must plan to stay in for at least eight years. They will actually retire in five years on a smaller budget, then transfer these high-growth assets to Tier Ones at around the time they turn sixty-eight.

Last week I got a call on my radio show from a former stockbroker who invested all his money in Tier-Three speculations. By 1984, when he was sixty, he was left with only $75,000. He completely tightened his belt ("no restaurants," he told my audience). He invested every penny he had and all new money in a variety of balanced and bond funds. Today, at age seventy, he has accumulated $550,000. He is eating in restaurants again! Such is the effect of a decade of diligence.

WHATEVER HAPPENED TO TIER-THREE INVESTING?

Tier-Three investing is there for the dollars that you can invest over and above what you need for your target goal. They are not "officially" part of your model portfolio. Add them when you are on your way or have arrived at your goal. There are, though, two major exceptions to this: gold and real estate. These can add considerably to your net worth if bought in the right economic time.

Let's look at ways to judge the economy so you can adjust your investments for maximum gain.

CHAPTER 14

How to Use Economic Signals to Make Up for Lost Time

An economist is like a man who knows everything about women,

but doesn't know any women.

ART BUCHWALD

Every major financial journal predicts the economic future for us, if only we are willing to look. With foresight we can adjust our Three-Tier portfolio from time to time. It has been my experience that even a cursory adjustment of an investment portfolio in light of economic change can result in as much as a 200 percent increase in wealth in a fifteen-year economic cycle. This means that if you are forty, you may do four times as well as your target goal by the time you retire at seventy if you are willing to receive guidance from economic predictors.

Using predictors is very easy. A large group of economic signals and indicators is used to construct three economic indexes: the Index of Leading Economic Indicators, the Index of Coincident Economic Indicators, and the Index of Lagging Economic Indicators. These herald changes in the economy before they happen and help us confirm the certainty of those changes. Only a few of the factors quantified in these indexes include

Employment rate
Household income
Use of credit
Retail prices
Production volume
Orders of durable goods
Government expenditures
Business revenue
Consumer spending
Balance of trade

Also, certain federal government policies tell us what's about to happen so we can make the best adjustments to our Three-Tier portfolio. Finally, we can use other, more minor indicators to confirm our conclusions. Let's look at how to use the indexes, changes in federal policy, and selected miscellaneous economic indicators to help us make up for lost time.

ECONOMIC INDICATOR INDEXES

THE INDEX OF LEADING ECONOMIC INDICATORS

The Index of Leading Economic Indicators lets you compare this month's economic trend with last month's. It's like a snapshot of the economy taken every month. It combines a number of signals, some of which are changes in inventory, prices of five hundred common stocks, and the number of new building permits issued. Some signals are provided in dollars adjusted for inflation; others are provided in physical units. The U.S. Department of Commerce weighs these signals and from them constructs the Index of Leading Economic Indicators. The index is published thirty days after the month analyzed and is reported in the television and radio financial news and in major financial newspapers.

Recessions are heralded by a downturn in the Index of Leading Economic Indicators, prosperity by an upturn, and expansion by a large surge. An upturn may be (but is not always) a signal that inflation is about to increase, often in proportion to the amount of the upturn.

THE INDEX OF COINCIDENT ECONOMIC INDICATORS

The Index of Coincident Economic Indicators analyzes different signals, for example, the gross national product, industrial production, employment, and personal income. Like the Index of Leading Economic Indicators, a downturn in this index heralds recession, an upturn better times and perhaps inflation. However, this index gives you *current* trends rather than leading or lagging trends.

Rule: If both indexes are in accord, a steady trend is confirmed. If they are at odds, we are at the beginning or end of a cycle.

So, when you see a divergence in the Leading and the Coincident indexes, it's time to review the investments you have made. For example, watching these indexes would have tipped you off to the recession of the late eighties.

THE INDEX OF LAGGING ECONOMIC INDICATORS

To fine-tune your assessment even more, look at the Index of Lagging Economic Indicators. The signals analyzed here include bank rates on short-term business loans, book value of inventory, labor costs per unit of manufacture, and business expenditure to expand plants. The figures of this index are made public slightly after a trend is spotted, to confirm the trend. They are useful to those who want to be sure about the certainty of these changes, even if it means being a little slow in reacting to them.

Rule: If this index is on a rise, an upward trend is confirmed. If it is on a downturn, after the Leading and Coincident Economic Indicators indexes show an upturn, that upturn may not last long.

USING THE INDEXES TO MAKE UP
FOR LOST TIME

Decisions regarding investments, moving, selling your house, making a large purchase, changing your career, or starting a business are all easier if you know how to read the economy.

Watch for these signs:

- Downturn in the Leading and Coincident indexes means a recession. If we are already in a recession, it means a worsening of the recession.
- Upturn in the Leading and Coincident indexes means a recovery. If we already are in a recovery, it means an expansion and perhaps inflation.
- Movement up or down in the Lagging index confirms the trend.

What if the indexes move in opposite directions?

- Downturn in the Leading index and an upturn in the Coincident index mean we are moving from expansion to recession. We are at the beginning of a downward spiral.
- Upturn in the Leading index and a downturn in the Coincident index mean a movement for the better; i.e., recession to recovery.
- The Lagging index will confirm the trend. A large fluctuation means that the trend will take hold quickly.

There is even a way to use the indexes to predict a change very early on. If you admire people who always buy or sell at the right time, don't attribute it to luck. They may be using the indexes to see that a recession bringing lower prices is about to occur, even in the midst of what appears to be a boom.

To do this yourself, do what economists do: When economists want to predict the future of a trend, they take the ratio of the Coincident to the Lagging index and compare it to the Leading index. When these are equal or negative during a rising trend, there is about to be a downturn, also called a recession. If the ratio is positive during a downward trend, there is about to be a recovery.

Luckily, you don't have to do any of this yourself. That's what economists are for. The ratio is published from time to time in the major economic journals, like *The Wall Street Journal* and *Barron's*. These publications obtain their figures from the *Federal Reserve Bulletin*, available at your local library.

FEDERAL POLICY

THE FED

Another important method of following economic trends is tracking the activities of the Federal Reserve System, known as the Fed. The Fed is in charge of tempering economic trends so they don't go wild. It is composed of twelve regional banks, twenty-five Federal Reserve branches, and all the national and state banks that are part of the Federal Reserve System. The chairman of the Fed is appointed by the President and confirmed by the Senate.

The Fed is mandated to keep us on an even economic keel. Its policy is supposed to act like the ballast of a ship, or like the intermediary between too much yin and too much yang. Poetic as that may sound, the Fed engages in hard-core money-supply manipulation of a startling nature. To understand how it does this, you must know that our money supply is measured in terms of M-1, M-2, and M-3.

M-1 is the national sum total of currency, checking account deposits, savings accounts, and nonbank traveler's checks. M-2 consists of the above plus commercial and other time deposits over $100,000 and repurchase agreements. M-3 adds T-bills, U.S. savings bonds, Eurodollars, banker's acceptances, and commercial paper to the M-2's provenance. Think of them, taken together, as the amount of money in the nation's wallet, ready for action.

When the nation has pulled back into recession or depression, there is precious little M-1, M-2, or M-3 around. In go-go years there is quite a lot. In inflationary times, there is too much. Then the Fed intervenes—in one of four ways:

1. By increasing or decreasing the amount of money a bank can lend by changing the amount of cash reserves the bank must maintain in proportion to the money it lends. If the bank needs to keep more on reserve, it lends less. Money becomes tight. This helps to rein in unchecked inflation.

2. By increasing or decreasing the discount rate (the rate charged to member banks to borrow money from the Fed). This raises and lowers the lending rates to nonmember banks and in turn to you. It also manipulates the amount of interest you receive on interest-bearing bank investments like certificates of deposit and savings accounts. Pretty soon, other institutions like municipalities and mortgage companies, which compete with banks in the borrowing and lending of money, change their rates to conform with the competition. In this way the Fed manipulates both the amount it costs you to borrow and the interest rates you get if you invest.

3. By increasing or decreasing the assets purchased from banks (like federal bonds owned by banks). This cash infusion increases the money supply. Cash held by banks can also be exchanged for bonds, thereby decreasing the money supply. All of these manipulations are performed by Federal Open Market Committee (FOMC). The FOMC meets in private and makes its decisions public six to eight weeks after the meeting.

4. By increasing the money supply by printing more money.

USING THE ACTIVITIES OF THE FED TO
MAKE UP FOR LOST TIME

As with the indexes, you can follow the activities of the Fed by reading and listening to financial news. Major libraries, including law libraries, also have copies of the *Federal Reserve Bulletin*.

Fed policy either loosens or tightens the money supply. A loose money supply means lower interest rates, more aggressive lending, and increased borrowing. A tight money supply will increase the prime rate (the rate charged by banks to commercial borrowers), and, again, the domino effect on interest rates takes place.

But that's not all. Stock prices are affected as money goes toward or away from interest rate investing. All in all, many economists believe that 70 percent of the price of a share of stock is affected by economic indicators and by the Fed's money policy rather than the soundness of the company. That means that *seventy cents of every dollar you put into stock is dictated by economic cycles.*

If the indexes herald a recession, you can expect that the Fed will eventually loosen the money supply. It will decrease the discount rate, decrease the reserve requirements, buy bank assets, or even print more money. Interest rates will fall, and stock buying will increase together with stock prices.

By contrast, in a recovery or inflation, Fed policy will tighten the money supply. Reserve requirements increase, as does the discount rate. Interest rates rise, and money may flow away from stock purchases to bonds.

MISCELLANEOUS ECONOMIC INDICATORS

ANNUAL GROWTH RATE

There is an additional method of understanding the economy that focuses only on the productivity and growth of business. This is called the Gross Annual Product. It is more helpful to us than the Gross National Product (GNP).

The GNP is the total of all goods produced for ultimate consumption (not as part of interim manufacture). Unfortunately, it is measured quarterly and yearly and therefore always gives us old news.

The GNP adjusted for inflation and other factors is released by the government as the Annual Growth Rate. Watch diligently for an annual growth rate of 6 percent. Historically, when the growth rate reaches that level, business change occurs. Above that level, downturns occur. Below that level, upturns occur, unless we are headed for a severe recession or depression. An annual growth rate of 9 percent almost guarantees a downturn, as history shows that this is a high growth rate to maintain.

We have already lived through eight recessions. If you had used the index method and watched the annual growth rate and the Fed, you could have acted rather than reacted to changing economic conditions and predicted the recessions of 1954–55, 1960–61, 1970–72, 1979–80, 1982, 1990–92.

ANOTHER INDEX THAT TIPS YOU OFF TO A COMING INFLATION

Inflation results in rising prices, so pay attention to the direction of the Consumer Price Index and the Producer Price Index (the costs to wholesalers). These rise and fall proportionately to inflation.

USING YOUR "CLAIRVOYANCE" TO MAKE UP FOR LOST TIME

As you follow the indexes, watch for the first sign that the Index to Leading Economic Indicators and the Index to Coincident Economic Indicators are not in accord, i.e., one has gone down and the other up since the last time you looked.

If the Leading is down and the Coincident is up from a prior month that you already checked, we may be moving toward recession. If this continues in each subsequent month so that the gap widens in a month or two, you have most likely confirmed a definite trend. Do the following:

- Lock in Tier-One interest rates. Choose long maturity dates, particularly in zero-coupon bonds. Most likely, interest rates will go down soon (then you can enjoy the higher rates or sell your bonds at a profit during the recession).
- Sell real estate that is not self-supporting, since the market will likely drop. Take your profit now.
- Sell recession-sensitive stocks like oil, auto, and industrials.
- Buy recession-proof stocks like drugs, food, and ecology.
- Keep profits in cash so you can buy low-priced real estate or stocks during the recession.

If the Leading is up and the Coincident is down, we are moving toward inflation. Here's what to do:

- Buy the real estate and stocks that you like now, since prices will be higher soon.
- Buy gold, art, tangibles, and other inflation fighters.
- Sell nothing: you'll make better profits later on.
- Don't lock in long maturity dates on Tier Ones.

IF YOU ARE A RISK TAKER

Follow the ratio of Coincident to Lagging economic indicators as compared to the Leading. If the ratio is negative, expect a trend toward recession and take the steps I advised for recession. If the ratio is positive, gear up for inflation. Since this is a very early indicator, you will be acting in a manner contrary to that of most investors. You must have a lot of self-confidence and the temperament of a risk taker, but the rewards can be great.

Always double-check your indicator predictions by watching the Fed. It will confirm your conclusions. If money policy is tight, the Fed is confirming inflation. If it is loose, the Fed is coping with recession.

Economic cycles can give you broad hints about whether to be bull (a buyer) or bear (a seller, or a sideliner). One key to making up for lost time is to act in anticipation of an economic change. Just before a new cycle takes hold, check your portfolio and adjust it accordingly. As the economy stabilizes, stay with the portfolio at hand and make changes only if your goals change or if a particular asset is not performing well.

CHAPTER 15

How and When to Pick a Financial Adviser Who Will Help You Make Up for Lost Time

The populace may hiss me, but when I go home and think of my money I applaud myself.

HORACE,
Epistles

Our image of financial professionals has changed through the years. In the past, brokers were professionals for the rich, making deals with a telephone at each ear. Mass marketing on a colossal scale now reaches out to the average person in an attempt to create an aura of comfort and credibility around financial advisers. That's not easy when memories of eighties tax shelter frauds, failed banks, and jailed Wall Street criminals still haunt us.

The reality is that a good financial professional can give you an invaluable extra edge in making up for lost time. But you must know how to find the best candidate for the job, what each type of professional can do for you, and what it will cost. The proper approach to using professional help in making up for lost time is to avoid the extremes of too much trust or too much suspicion. Instead, to get maximum results, use professionals wherever you can, but always be an active participant in the decision-making process.

I am a lawyer, financial planner, and tax consultant, and I have an insurance license and a series 7 brokerage license. Except for my lawyer's license, I have permitted all the others to lapse so that I could keep objectivity. Although I am no longer licensed, as a former salesperson in so many areas of personal finance, I have an inside view of how best to use professionals to make up for lost time.

First: Take Responsibility

Buyer's remorse is unbecoming to you. You're not a baby anymore; it's wrong to blame the broker when you were misled by your own greed or indolence. Buy investments when you know what you want and why. If you're happy to take the credit for your profits, you must be prepared to take responsibility for your losses.

Don't ever "be sold" an investment. Buy it. The difference is simple. You are sold an investment when the need to buy it is implanted in you by a self-interested salesperson, without regard to your overall needs. You buy an investment when you have focused on your needs and then make your own selection with the salesperson's advice. If you give someone else control and that investment fails, you'll complain, "He never should have sold it to me." *Take responsibility before you buy instead of blaming others afterward.* You'll have a lot less to complain about, and you'll make a lot more money that way.

Second: Keep a Watchful Eye on All Transactions

Use a tape recorder and follow up your conversations with sales people (planners, brokers, insurance agents) with letters, despite the temptation to let the phone do your work. Let your financial adviser know that you are making a record of your conversations and following up with a written confirmation. Your purpose is to avoid misunderstanding, so how can he or she object?

THIRD: BE ALERT TO INNOVATION

While they are not always the top performers, there are enough excellent no-load (no commission) mutual funds available so that you can make an investment without paying a commission. As of this writing, a new type of fund is on the horizon. The fund is sold to you by a licensed broker, but you pay no load. Instead, the broker gets a commission from the company based on the performance of the fund over the years. The idea is to build a sales force committed to the product. Will it attract brokers? Will it attract investors? There should be only one criterion: how well the fund itself will do. Learn about brand-new innovations such as these, but invest very little in any innovation that has a short track record. When the results over time warrant it, you may increase your investment.

FOURTH: KNOW THE CAST OF CHARACTERS

It pays to know the many types of financial professionals there are and what they can do for you.

PROFESSIONALS WHO OFFER TAX HELP

Accountants give tax advice and help in tax preparation.

Certified Public Accountants do what accountants do, and can represent you before the IRS. They usually specialize in more sophisticated planning than accountants do.

Tax Attorneys do all of the above plus prepare legal documents that are part of a business or sophisticated tax plan. They can also represent you in tax court if an IRS dispute gets that far.

Enrolled Agents do tax planning, prepare returns, and represent you before the IRS. They have to have worked at the IRS for five years before going into private practice.

Bookkeepers keep monthly track of your credit cards and bills and balance your checkbook. An accountant can supply a bookkeeper. Whomever you use, have the bookkeeper check in with the accountant four times a year to be sure that your file is complete.

All of these professionals charge on an hourly basis for their work. The range is vast, from as little as $6 an hour for a self-trained bookkeeper to $500 an hour for a tax attorney in a big city. Ask what the fee is before you sit down for a consultation. Get friends and relatives to refer you to professionals they respect. Chat about the professionals' clientele and major strengths. Read the wall (see the schools they attended and when).

PROFESSIONALS WHO EXECUTE STOCK AND BOND TRADES

Brokers are middlemen. They are licensed to buy investments for you that you are not allowed to buy on your own. Brokers make money only if you buy or sell. That gives them a strong incentive to make sure you buy. Often, if your account is inactive, they will try to persuade you to sell. Be very wary of a broker who "pushes" you to sell or to buy. There is a commission in it for the broker, as well as the potential of a new sale when you decide to reinvest after selling.

In the past, brokers were just product salesmen. The new breed of broker is also an adviser with a financial-planning bent. I predict that someday the industry will reward brokers on more than just sales. Already some firms boost a broker's earnings if customers are retained over long periods of time, presumably satisfied with their portfolios' performance.

Brokers are employed by a member firm of the National

Association of Securities Dealers (NASD). That organization can provide information on the status of brokers, handle complaints against them, and hold arbitrations if you have a claim.

Full-Service Brokers is a new name for ordinary brokers to distinguish them from discount brokers. Full-service brokers receive research reports based on in-house analysis. These reports can be unreliable when the company headquarters is motivating its brokers to sell certain types of investments. Sometimes, headquarters is beholden to a company making a stock offering, so brokers are given research that is slanted in favor of an offering. Sometimes a broker will simply offer the product that generates the highest commissions. Commissions can range from twelve cents a share for those actively traded to fifty cents a share for over-the-counter stock (sold from an issuer not on the stock exchange). Find out what your broker is charging by asking what he or she will earn from the transaction, not what you will pay (often there are hidden benefits like a free trip to Hawaii or a bonus associated with certain high-commission products). You are entitled to view his or her level of compensation as a measure of his or her self-interest.

A broker may not be deliberately misleading you. Often the high-commission product is one for which the brokerage house provided a seminar and a set of materials that cause the broker to give it extra attention and sales effort. All in all, I do not believe that relying solely on a broker will do the job. You are likely to end up with scattered investments that do not follow a well-thought-out plan.

Therefore, you should use a broker just to execute the trades if you are sophisticated enough to proceed without help (see *Discount Brokers* and *Deep-Discount Brokers*). If you need advice, use a broker who will pay attention to your overall plan and will focus in the area you request. To be fair, I know many excellent brokers of this type. Many are my television and radio sponsors. This is how they distinguish themselves from the others:

- They plan with you.
- They understand your tax needs.
- They know what else you own.
- They respect your risk level.
- They explain a complex investment.
- They write their own bulletins for clients as well as sending you the company newsletter.

Discount Brokers are brokers whose primary service is to make trades. Using a discount broker, you can save over 50 percent on commissions as compared to when you use a full-service broker, according to a sliding scale based on the amount of the purchase. Discount brokers may not do research and planning, or offer special conveniences like checking attached to your money market account, but many do; you must ask. They do provide margin accounts, consolidated statements, and pension accounts just like full-service brokers. Many also will purchase no-load mutual funds for you and for a small fee (usually $25 a year) will send you a monthly consolidated statement of your no-load funds.

If you're interested in the Tier-Three strategy of buying investments on margin, bear in mind that not all discount brokers welcome margin buyers. If you go with a full-service broker for margin investing, don't use the high-commission broker for your other trades unless you are a good enough customer to be able to reduce commissions from a full-service broker.

Deep-Discount Brokers just take orders and have (not surprisingly) the lowest commission charge. Some deep-discount brokers require a cash account, so you cannot buy on margin. They charge a flat fee instead of a percentage of the purchase price, and the commissions are based on the number, not the cost, of shares. For example: A deep-discount broker may charge an $8.00 service fee per trade plus $35.00 for 100 to 3,000 shares; $50.00 for 3,100 to 5,000 shares; $0.01 per share over $5,000.

PLANNERS

Registered Investment Advisors (RIAs) give advice on investing under the Registered Investment Advisor Act of 1940. RIAs do not need a license, but a very stringent filing requirement regarding their own finances and way of doing business is required. They are under yearly review from the Securities Exchange Commission. RIAs are strictly fee-paid advisers, taking no commission unless they also have a separate broker's license. Some act as money managers (see below). RIAs set an hourly rate and are compensated much like attorneys for their time.

Money Managers make financial decisions for you under a contract that lasts for a period of time, usually a year or two. You can test a money manager by asking him or her to accept a test portfolio. Usually a money manager will insist on a test portfolio of at least $50,000, although you may be able to test for as low as $25,000. If you try it, the money manager will need at least a year, often two, in order to show his or her stuff.

As compensation, the money manager earns a percentage of the money you place under management, anywhere between 1 and 4 percent. The money manager will trade your account through a broker to implement investment decisions, and he or she usually has a discount arrangement with the broker.

Money managers should *not* be

Commissioned salespeople, including brokers, insurance agents, or financial planners with selling licenses.

Nonprofessionals who have done well for themselves and think they can do well for you while they pursue their main career.

A money manager should

Tailor the portfolio for you alone, not adhere to a generic portfolio.

Provide printed materials that clearly define his or her investing philosophy, which should be one that you can understand, and agree with.

Provide a prediction of performance that is realistic, consistent with past performance, and quoted based on the size of the portfolio that you are contemplating. A small portfolio will not perform as well as a large one over time. You should not rely on past performance based on handling $500,000 if you intend to invest $50,000.

Have an investment philosophy that combines quality, diversification, and a balance of growth and income, all undertaken at the risk level acceptable to you.

Financial Planners gather data regarding your goals and prepare a program that provides a blueprint of how different investments will function to meet the goal. No license is required, but many have received certification as a Certified Financial Planner (CFP) from a correspondence school in Denver, which has its trademark on the certificate. I have seen the materials and exams. They are well-thought-out and difficult. To find out if your planner is a graduate, contact the International Board of Standards and Practices for Certified Financial Planners, 1660 Lincoln Street, Denver, CO 80264, or call 303-830-7543.

Some financial planners are Registered Financial Planners (RFPs). This is a title conferred by the International Association of Registered Financial Planners, a trade association located in El Paso, TX (1-800-749-7947).

I was a member of the regional board of the International Association of Financial Planners, an important national trade association for planners. For information, its address is 119 West Fortieth Street, New York, NY 10018.

The notion of having a financial planner is very popular these days. People want to see clearly what they are investing in and why. As a result, many personal finance professionals want to be called financial planners. Insurance agents, brokers, and tax professionals all get into the act, since there is no separate licensing for planners and anyone can hang up a shingle. Many banks are opening up financial-planning departments. There are even New Age planners whose backgrounds are as psychics.

Given the wide-open opportunity to be misled, choose a financial planner who has been in the business for at least ten years or who works for a company that has. Pick one who charges a reasonable fee for a well-done plan. Ask to see a sample plan first and talk honestly about the software he or she uses. Ask if he or she is also licensed to sell products, and if so, whose? The more freedom the financial planner has to sell a large range of products, the better. If the financial planner works, for a company that creates its own products, ask to see the line so you can evaluate its performance before you use its services.

Sometimes a financial planner will do a lot of original work for free. It's usually to make a sale. Let your conscience be your guide if you take up a lot of time with no intention of buying.

PROFESSIONALS WHO HANDLE LOANS

Personal Bankers are bank officers who know people personally and who help them with loans and business needs. Bankers can also be licensed to sell annuities and mutual funds, and to act as brokers. The people who do the selling are not only personal bankers, they are also separately licensed salespeople. In that capacity, they are often working for the brokerage subsidiary of the bank. Pick a bank for the services it gives to its depositors, i.e., business loans and full- or low-cost checking. Use a bank that makes loan applications and rates more favorable for those who bank there. Convenience of location is important, but before long most banking will be electronic. Accurate record keeping and low fees are more appealing than a high-cost, low-service bank on the corner. Never confuse the bank's brokerage arm with its banking arm.

They are two different enterprises operating in the same building.

FIDUCIARIES

Fiduciaries, Agents, and Treuhands are professionals of any variety who act as trustees. Treuhands are foreign fiduciaries who hold your assets in other countries.

The full scope of trust placed in these professionals is enormous. Many banks and attorneys act in this capacity. Depending on the trust document, the fiduciary may even be making the investments or choosing the broker who does. Ask for and check out a referral from the attorney who creates the trust, and always meet the fiduciary in his or her office for in-depth discussion. Fees are usually based on a percentage of the amount in the trust and follow a sliding scale from 2 to 5 percent (the larger the amount, the smaller the percentage).

Insurance Agents sell insurance. Today most agents are also licensed to sell mutual funds, annuities, and other investments. Many agents are Chartered Life Underwriters (CLUs), which means that they have completed a course at the American College in Pennsylvania. They may also be Chartered Financial Consultants (ChFCs), signifying that they completed a correspondence course from the same school. (See Chapter 21 for my thoughts on selecting an insurance company.)

FOR THE DO-IT-YOURSELFER

Even if you use no-load mutual funds to a large extent, a time will come when you will want to purchase a stock or zero-coupon bond or trade an option. The law requires that you use a broker. Know what you want to buy first. Then shop for the lowest commission. Use a discount broker, a number of no-load mutual funds, and a convenient bank. That's all. If you want to buy some individual stocks, buy through Dividend Reinvestment Plans (DRIPs). Most major companies will sell stock in their corporation directly to you. For a list, write to Dow Theory Forecasts, Inc., 7412 Calumet Avenue, Hammond, IN 43624-2692, or call 219-931-6480.

Of course, a do-it-yourselfer must read books and newsletters, and even go to seminars. A good place to start is the Bibliography at the back of this book.

PART IV

Yours and Theirs and Theirs: How to Handle the Triple Squeeze of Your Retirement, Your Children's College, and Your Parents' Needs

CHAPTER 16

A Menu of Pension Plans

The future ain't what it used to be.

YOGI BERRA

In the triple squeeze of financial goals—retirement, college, and helping your parents—retirement must take priority. Consider the parallel to airplane crash survival. In the event of lack of oxygen in the cabin, put your mask on first. You cannot help others if you are in trouble yourself.

Moreover, it's easiest to make up for lost time with tax-deferred investing. Only retirement programs protected by the IRS, private annuities, and certain insurance policies allow you to tax-defer.

At this time, tax deferral is a powerful tool to wealth building. You pay no income tax on the interest, capital gain, or other profit from an investment held in a tax-deferred vehicle. That means that all your money is reinvested for you. The amount in taxes you would ordinarily pay is still in your account and earning dollars for you.

If the account is a tax-deferred pension plan, you have also deferred the taxes on the deposits in the year you earn them. There never used to be any controversy as to the value of such tax deferral. Now there is.

If your tax bracket in your earning years is lower than it will be in your retirement and you are ten years or less from retirement, there is a slim chance, based on many complicated factors, that you'll do better paying the tax and investing tax-exempt. However, this is only the case if your employer doesn't contribute to your pension plan.

For most Americans, their tax-deferred pension is the quickest vehicle to make up for lost time. Today, these pensions are largely deferred-compensation plans, to which you can voluntarily contribute and even control with the Three-Tier method.

The defined-benefit plan, the "old-fashioned" pension—in which the employer alone paid in, controlled the investment, and doled out a lifetime of monthly checks—is rapidly being replaced by the 401(k)s and other deferred-contribution plans available today. More and more, it is you who are responsible for disciplined pension investing and asset selection. This chapter will explain your choices.

Those of you with defined-benefit plans don't have much control over them, but you should investigate their safety. With all the talk about problems with Social Security, it's not unreasonable to be suspicious of pension safety. Let's start with the fundamental question: How safe is your pension?

Prediction: Many corporate pension plans are insured by a government-created corporation named the Pension Benefits Guarantee Corporation (PBGC). The PBGC is underfunded by $51 billion. The agency is running a deficit of $2.3 billion. PBGC head Joseph Delfico has reported to the House labor-management subcommittee that there is cash flow to pay present obligations for up to two years. It is likely that you will be reading this book just as the full impact of the pension deficit, affecting 41 million workers and their families, is felt.

My prediction is that these pensions will be saved by the government, which means all of us as taxpayers will bear the burden. I also predict that, like Social Security, there will be new restrictions that will affect those of us retiring around and after the year 2000.

Another safety issue involves the choice of investment. Many pensions of all varieties are invested in guaranteed investment contracts (GICs). These are fixed-income products with guaranteed interest rates. They are all Tier Ones with a problem: While the interest is guaranteed, the principal is not. At least two major insurance companies have defaulted on GICs. Pension managers have a new awareness of the problem and are more careful; and many are considering a new product called a bank investment contract (BIC), issued by banks.

GIC safety is not to be taken lightly. If the insurance company issuing the contract goes under, the investment may not pay off. Many conservative workers elected GICs in the belief that these were the safest type of pension investment. They gave up both a chance to make up for lost time and the safety they sought.

If you have a GIC, it is most likely in your 401(k). If so, you may be able to change it to a Tier Two. That is most likely the better investment to make up for lost time, anyway. If your GIC is giving you a handsome interest rate, check the safety of the company that issued it by using the pointers in Chapter 21.

Let's look at the different types of pension plans.

DEFINED-BENEFIT PLAN

A defined-benefit plan pays a fixed (usually monthly) income at your retirement for the rest of your life. The company takes the risk of your longevity: Certain options permit you to extend the pension to the life of your spouse or other beneficiary. The pension is managed by the group chosen by your employer. The amount you receive depends on salary and length of service. *The employer makes all the investment decisions, but if they go wrong, you get the full pension anyway.*

TIPS FOR USING DEFINED-BENEFIT PLANS TO MAKE UP FOR LOST TIME

Know the formula upon which your company bases the benefit. If it is a percentage of your average career salary, you might be better off earning moderate amounts each year instead of very little for a number of years and then a big jump at the end of your work life. This could lead to a higher average.

By contrast, other plans base the formula on a percentage of earnings in the last five years you work, multiplied by the number of years of service. Under this kind of formula, you are best off with job longevity and a big sprint in income at the end of your work life.

If you intend to stay in your job, know the pension's rules. If you are looking for employment, you can judge a job's pension program based on how these different formulas fit into your future work life.

If you plan to make up for lost time with a new job or career, you may forfeit the pension from the job you leave unless the pension is "vested" (became yours to take with you because you worked the required number of years).

Full vesting, called Cliff vesting, requires five years of employment. Then you are fully vested. Partial vesting requires three years of work. After that you are vested at the rate of 20 percent each year until you are fully vested. Bear in mind that vesting in any moneys *you* contributed is immediate.

A friend of mine is living apart from her husband with their eight-month-old son because her husband was transferred out of state one year before her pension vested. She made the right decision. The strain of separation will be handsomely rewarded by a lifetime of pension benefits.

Even if it has vested, an interrupted plan costs you money. If you change jobs after age forty, try to negotiate a bonus in the form of an extra pension contribution that makes up for the pension loss that leaving your old job may engender.

If you leave with a vested pension, you may, under limited circumstances, be able to roll it over into an individual retirement account (IRA) (see page 159) or your new plan. On rare occasions, it is best to leave the pension under the administration of the former employer. This is so when the employer is a large, solid company and the amount projected to be received at retirement is more than you believe the new employer or your own managed IRA can accumulate for you.

Maternity leave, or leaving for another job and returning to the old one, may not disqualify you from keeping your pension credits. Get the details from the company's employee benefits department.

Since a defined-benefit plan is entirely under the direction of an employer, many employees don't know their benefits until right before retirement. To find out where you stand, meet with the employee benefits department of your firm. Read the "survivor coverage" data to find out your spouse's rights. Keep up with your yearly benefits statement.

Some plans are "integrated with Social Security." This means that your employer can contribute less to your pension depending on how much Social Security contribution was made. You are entitled to a report of the integration formula, as well as to an understanding of any cost-of-living adjustments made to the pension formula. One excellent way of dealing with inflation is to join a company that adjusts its pension to a valid cost-of-living index.

If you have your own business, a wonderful technique for making up for lost time is to create a defined-benefit plan. It allows you to contribute to fund a targeted benefit.

If you have fewer than fifteen years until retirement and own your own business, get in touch with a pension planner. The defined-benefit plan allows you to exclude certain employees, to integrate Social Security (thereby reducing the amount you must contribute on behalf of employees), and to set your maximum retirement goals. *Caution: Once you have fixed a benefit, you must make the contribution that meets it regardless of the profit of your company.*

DEFINED-CONTRIBUTION PLAN

A defined-contribution plan has no targeted retirement goal. The employer contributes to the pension each year. With some types of defined-contribution plans, like the 401(k), the employee can contribute too. The amount contributed can change each year depending on the type of plan it is, and it is contributed to your individual account. You are often asked to choose among investments that fall into the Three Tiers we have already discussed. You will retire on less if you make wrong choices.

The defined-contribution plan is not insured, and contributions are limited to $30,000 or 25 percent of your annual pay, whichever is less.

TIPS ON MAKING UP FOR LOST TIME WITH YOUR DEFINED-CONTRIBUTION PLAN

Sock away every penny you are entitled to contribute.

Integrate your investment decisions into the Three-Tier system. That will mean a high percentage in long-term equities and a lower percentage in the fixed-income choices if you are eight or more years from retirement.

Know the difference between the types of defined-contribution plans outlined below, and pick your next job accordingly. If you own your own business, set the right one up for yourself.

TYPES OF DEFINED-CONTRIBUTION PLANS:

401(k)

401(k)s have a number of attractive features:

- Automatic vesting of your contribution.
- Gradual vesting of your employer's contribution.
- If you leave, you can roll it over to an IRA or to a new 401(k).
- For the most part, you will dictate how the money is invested by choosing among a variety of mutual fund choices. Use the Three-Tier system to make your decision.
- You can borrow up to $50,000 from a 401(k) and pay yourself back with interest based on the interest charged by banks to corporate borrowers.
- Some 401(k)s permit purchases of your company's stock. Consider this a Tier-Two investment. Another variation is an ESOP, a plan that allows you to buy only company stock. This is also a Tier Two, with no diversification. Nevertheless, it's tax-deferred. Do it as long as you can diversify in other ways and your company is strong.

Your employer can set aside up to 25 percent of your compensation or $30,000 a year, whichever is less. You can set aside up to approximately $9,000 a year or a maximum percentage of your salary in a 401(k). The figures change slightly each year, so check with your financial adviser. If you work for a school, hospital, or nonprofit group, you get a 403(b), which brings the amount up to $9,500.

You designate an amount to be deducted automatically from your salary. You are not taxed on it in the year you earn it, although Social Security is taken out. To make up for lost time, contribute every penny you can and ask whether you can contribute more than the maximum amount in after-tax contributions. At least you will be earning subsequent interest and gains tax-deferred.

If your employer matches your contribution, grab the opportunity and fund to the max!

Profit-Sharing Plan

Another variation on the theme of defined-contribution plans is the profit-sharing plan. This is a streamlined plan where employees direct their own investments and get immediate vesting, and contributions are purely discretionary on the part of the employer. If you are an employee and this is all you have, don't count on much without a lot of luck and a generous employer. However, the employer can place up to 15 percent of your salary or $30,000, whichever is less, in your pension.

Money-Purchase Plan

This plan is similar to a profit sharing, but the employer must select a specific annual contribution, usually a percentage of the employee's salary. The contribution must be the same percentage each year regardless of profits. As with the defined-benefit plan, know your company's policy. The percentage can be anywhere from 1 to 25 percent or $30,000, whichever is less.

A Combination Plan If You Are Self-Employed

Many businesspeople would do best by setting up a corporation and combining a money-purchase and profit-sharing plan. Lock in the required money-purchase amount at 10 percent and retain the 15 percent discretionary profit-sharing plan. In this way, the combined contribution allowed is $30,000 or 25 percent of your net earned income as shown on Schedule C of your income tax return, less the amount you are contributing to the retirement account (whichever is less). If the year isn't so good, you must contribute the 10 percent required under the money-purchase, but you can stay flexible on the other 15 percent contributed under the profit-sharing plan.

If you are your own employee, you can make up for lost time by socking away as much as you can using this combination, without having to commit yourself to too much in off years.

WHATEVER HAPPENED TO THE KEOGH?

A self-employed person or a person with a job and additional income from self-employment can set up a defined-benefit Keogh, a defined-contribution Keogh, a profit-sharing Keogh, or a purchase-money Keogh. The paperwork is slightly different from that of corporate plans, and there may be no allowance to borrow against your money or to buy life insurance in your account. Otherwise, the old divergent rules between corporate and self-employed pensions are largely nonexistent today.

Most self-employed people set up a *defined-benefit Keogh*. This is a good choice if you have few employees and a large income, and are older than your employees. The best way to make up for lost time is to open a defined-benefit plan and contribute the maximum.

If, however, you choose the *defined-contribution plan*, you may select the money-purchase-plan variety. In that case, a contribution is made based on a percentage of the employee's (your) salary. You, as employer, may put up to 25 percent of income or $30,000 each year, whichever is less, into your Keogh plan. In addition, you may select a *profit-sharing plan* permitting up to a 15 percent contribution. This is a discretionary contribution, which gives you flexibility in an off year.

If you like the flexibility of the profit-sharing plan but don't want to limit yourself to a 15 percent contribution cap, you may decide to try the *combination plan* for corporations (page 156).

As with all tax-deferred programs, the earlier in the year you contribute, the sooner you start earning on your contribution. But you can start a Keogh with a small contribution and make the rest anytime before April 15 of the following year. For example, let's say you open the Keogh on December 15, 1993, with a contribution of $100. You can then put in up to the cap by April 15, 1994. In that case, you can deduct the combined amount from your 1993 income tax.

Cautions: You must make periodic reports to the government. This is usually done by your Keogh administrator—which is often you. Like any pension plan, the Keogh must be opened by the employer. So, if you have a partner, both of you must open the plan.

Just in case you are numbed by the rules, take a break and think of this scenario: You are forty, own your own business, and have no pension. Now you decide to contribute $15,000 each year to a Keogh, shooting for late retirement at age seventy-five. You get a realistic 8 percent on your investment. You retire with $2,741,532. If you use your Three-Tier system to average 10 percent, you'll retire with $4,471,901. Feel better?

A BIG PENSION BENEFIT FOR THE LITTLE GUY

If your company has no pension, ask your employer to set up a simplified employee pension (SEP). All that he or she need do is open an IRA for each individual employee. You are immediately vested with any contribution, and each employee directs his or her own investments. Best of all, there is almost no paperwork for your boss.

If your company has twenty-five employees or less, and at least

50 percent agree to contribute, you can make payroll deduction contributions. These contributions are tax-deductible and can be as much as $8,728 (this figure is indexed and goes up every year) or 15 percent of salary, whichever is less. If your employer is also contributing, the combined contribution cannot exceed 15 percent of salary.

Although your yearly contribution is discretionary, in order to make up for lost time it goes without saying that you should contribute. As with 401(k) employee contributions, Social Security payments are taken out of your salary even though the contributed portion is not included in your income. You can control the investments, and you are fully vested the moment the contribution is made.

So if Scrooge is your boss, point out the following about a SEP:

- The employer need not make any contributions.
- If the employer does contribute, it is a deductible business expense.
- You can contribute the difference between the employer's contribution and 15 percent of your salary up to the dollar maximum for the year.
- You can also contribute an additional $2,000 as an IRA contribution and combine your IRA and SEP accounts.

If you are self employed, need flexibility, and have few or no employees to whom you must give a pension benefit, SEP is the choice for you. Administration of SEP is a piece of cake! There are, however, some downsides that are often minimized by financial advisers:

- You can't buy life insurance with the plan. If you need insurance for a buy-out agreement, or to cover your heirs, you must pay with after-tax dollars.
- You can't roll your SEP over into an employer's plan. If you intend to get a job with an employer-run pension, you will have to continue to administer your own SEP.

- You cannot make a lump sum withdrawal at retirement and income-average to reduce the tax impact.

Most important, since contributions to SEPs are discretionary each year, you may become lax in making contributions. That's no way to make up for lost time.

To offset all these, remember that you can contribute after age seventy and a half to a SEP, which is great for us late bloomers!

IRA—WHAT HAS YOUR IRA DONE FOR YOU LATELY?

The individual retirement account (IRA) is a simple tax-deferred way of investing using the Three-Tier system. I'd like to bring back the heyday of the IRA, which ended in 1987 when the across-the-board deductibility rule was curtailed.

In the good old days, up to $2,000 a year of earned income per wage earner (or $2,250 for a married couple where one partner did not work) could be placed in an IRA. The amount deposited was not taxable income in the year earned. On the contrary, the taxpayer deducted his or her IRA contribution from earned income the year of the deposit. So not only was the future gains tax-deferred, but income tax was reduced by the tax on the deductible $2,000 contribution!

The IRA fell from grace in 1987 when complicated rules made the IRA nondeductible to some. However, many of you will still be able to take a deduction for your IRA contribution if

You and your spouse have no pension plan, regardless of income

You or your spouse is a member of a plan, and your combined "modified adjusted gross income" is $40,000 or less

You are covered by a plan, are single, and your modified adjusted gross income is $25,000 or less

If you earn more than the amounts described above, the deductibility of your contribution decreased by $200 for each additional $1,000 of income.

If you earn more than $50,000 of modified adjusted gross income as a couple or $35,000 as a single, your deduction phases out completely.

I urge those who can to take advantage of this extra deductible account, to best make up for lost time. Even those who can't take advantage of the tax breaks, however, should not pass up socking money away. It's easy to open an IRA: Any bank, mutual fund, or brokerage house can do it for you.

Every investment contained in the Three-Tier system will qualify for tax deferral on gains if bought in an IRA, with the following exceptions:

Art

Antiques

Collectibles

Coins, except for some U.S.-minted or state-minted coins

HOW TO GET THE MOST FROM YOUR IRA

If you really want to get the most from your IRA, fund it as early in the year as you can. However, if you are tardy, you can make contributions up to April 15 of the year after you earned the money. In fact, if you file early and get a refund, as long as it is before April 15, you can even use your tax refund money to make the contribution. The Internal Revenue Code allows qualifying individuals to take a deduction for their IRA contribution even if they have not made it as yet, as long as they meet the deadline.

Don't concern yourself with the fact that you cannot borrow from your IRA. Important legislation is pending at the time of this writing that would permit you to use IRA money for things like tuition or a first house. Start an IRA and write your congressperson in favor of the legislation.

Why bother? Because it gives everyone, without exception, an extra vehicle for making tax-deferred investments. Maybe one year you will be able to fund all other retirement vehicles to the hilt.

Good for you. An additional place to invest up to $4,000 for a working couple, tax-deferred, couldn't hurt.

TAX-DEFERRED ANNUITIES

You may have an inheritance, a capital gain, or a bit of lottery luck. Or you may be ferociously trying to make up for lost time and have funded every pension vehicle in sight. Now, how do you get tax deferral on your investments with unearned dollars, or dollars above your pension limits? Enter the tax-deferred annuity.

If I ruled the insurance industry, I would do two things with tax-deferred annuities. First, I would give them a new name so as to stop confusion with immediate annuities, which are deals you make with an insurance company to take your principal in return for a fixed monthly income for life. They have their place with older people who cannot manage money, as an alternative to a trust for adult incompetents, and to give peace of mind to those who are afraid they will outlive their finances. Even sales brochures sometime mix up the two types of annuities, because insurance companies sell both.

Second, I would make a bigger effort to sell tax-deferred annuities to younger people with extra assets. Why? Because once you have enough money to fund all your pension options to the hilt, and you have fifteen to twenty years before retirement, you need the tax-deferred annuity to make up for lost time.

THIRTEEN RULES FOR USING AN ANNUITY TO MAKE UP FOR LOST TIME

1. Fund all other tax-deferred vehicles first—even your $2,000 IRA.
2. Check out the insurance company behind the annuity. (See Chapter 21 on how to do that.)
3. Buy a variable-rate annuity if you are going to use the annuity for Tier-Two investing. A variable annuity func-

tions like a family of mutual funds with various growth goals. Use the same allocation you decided upon in your tier-system strategy.

4. *Check the past performance of the annuity just as you would a mutual fund: Read the prospectus.* There are 2,600 insurance companies. Most sell annuities. Diversify by owning several.

5. If you are buying an annuity as a Tier-One investment (i.e., as a stable source of income), check its past income-paying record. It's all in the company computer from day one. Don't fall for the high initial rate that is used to entice a new client. The renewal rates are often much lower one year later. In most cases, you can lock in a rate for from three to seven years.

6. Remember all the Tier-One rules. If the income fluctuates without certainty (indexed rates, variable rates, or floating rates), this is not a Tier-One investment. You are turning a Tier One into a Tier Three without the leverage that makes Tier Threes worthwhile. Finally, compare Tier-One annuities with other Tier Ones in the usual way (see page 79).

7. Look for an annuity that gives you unlimited free changes in your portfolio composition and offers at least seven different funds (most do).

8. Never buy an annuity with a front-end load. Few have one. Almost all have reasonable maintenance fees, paid yearly. All have exit fees if you leave early, usually before seven years. Further, all have an insurance component that costs money. The annuity company ensures that your heirs will receive at least the amount that you put in. This costs you between 0.5 and 1.5 percent per year. The Vanguard Annuity Plan, which is basically an index fund, charges a total of .87 percent a year for all expenses combined.

9. Except for these exit or redemption fees, you can switch your annuity from one company to another without adverse tax, cost, or penalty.

10. Make sure you can withdraw at least 10 percent of the principal each year without surrender fees. An annuity with this feature should be easy to find.

11. The tax rules for withdrawing annuities are about the same as those for withdrawing from pensions.

12. Beware of the annuity wrapper and other fees. Variable annuities can be costly even without a traditional front-end load.

   The yearly cost can be as much as 2.55 percent of the amount in the annuity. The tax savings resulting from deferral must exceed that cost. They will do so only if you are in at least the 28 percent bracket. If you are in a low tax bracket, you may be best off paying the taxes and buying the right mutual fund instead of a tax-deferred annuity.

13. Don't get starry-eyed over a printout predicting the future accumulation of the annuity unless it takes into account eventual taxes and fees through the years, and is based on past performance, not wishful thinking.

Despite the need for consumer awareness, annuities are one of your best (and most underutilized) bets for making up for lost time. If I could convey any one single idea to you from all I have included in this book, it is this: Fund your pensions and buy annuities with the rest of your retirement savings. Track your variable annuities in *Barron's*, which publishes a weekly report submitted by Lipper Analytic Services. Before you buy, check with Variable Annuity Research and Data Services (1-800-252-4600), which reports on the total return of over seven hundred annuity funds and takes costs into consideration.

INSURANCE AS A PENSION ALTERNATIVE

At present, insurance is a heavily tax-favored type of investment. Because of the tax aspects of insurance listed below, it is possible to use insurance as an addition or as an alternative to a pension. Let's see how this works, and then let's review the pros and cons.

INSURANCE TAX FACTS

1. Part of your insurance premiums are invested by the company in separate accounts, segregated for you, if you purchase "universal or variable life insurance." The earnings are tax-deferred, as with any pension or annuity

2. As the cash value of your policy increases (investments build through the years), you can withdraw up to the amount of the premiums you put in 100 percent tax-free. The IRS considers these withdrawals as return of your capital, not as a withdrawal of capital gains. After you withdraw all the premiums, the next dollar withdrawn is taxable.

3. You can borrow against your insurance policy cash value tax-free. The death benefit for your family is diminished by the loan amount.

Pros

These three tax facts lend themselves to the wise choice of using insurance as a method of tax-deferred investing for retirement, and using the proceeds of the investments tax-free when you retire.

In addition, you can contribute a premium that you determine without regard to ERISA laws (the federal statutes that control pension requirements) or IRS pension limitations. If you employ workers, you don't need to make any contributions for them, establish any separate trust fund, and file any cumbersome pension or administrative plans. You can make withdrawals at any time in your life penalty-free—you needn't wait until age fifty-nine and a half.

Perhaps the most remarkable thing about insurance as a pension alternative is the freedom you have to design the program. The only caveat about taxes is that if you pay in additional premiums over and above the amount necessary to fund the death benefit, the policy is taxable as an endowment rather than as an insurance policy. But the rules of overfunding still permit you to contribute far more than the death-benefit premium, and far more than the $30,000 a year cap for 401(k)s and other pension programs. Further, if your boss does not want to institute a pension, and your fellow employees don't agree on a SEP, you can autonomously create your own insurance program. Finally, if you are the Scrooge, you can put tax-free money away without setting up any contributory plan for your employees.

Cons

Although insurance policies allow you to contribute beyond the amount that is required to support the death benefit, the amount contributed is not tax-deductible from your income, unlike pension, IRA, SEP, and 401(k) contributions. If you are a business owner, your corporation can pay premiums for you and deduct the cost, but this income must be reported by you on your personal return. Check with your accountant to determine whether the corporate deduction is a benefit, considering the personal inclusion. In all other cases, the insurance premiums are nondeductible.

The premiums are invested depending on what type of policy you buy: whole life, variable life, or universal life. You'll find discussions of all three in Chapter 21. I am listing the investment aspect of these policies under "Cons" because it's my opinion that the investment return of many of these policies does not compare with that of self-directed pensions.

Further, a portion of your premium is going to support the death benefit in the policy. Most of you will borrow or withdraw enough of the cash value to make the eventual death benefit small. Therefore, these policies often cannot support the double function of providing a retirement benefit and a sizable death benefit. If you build up a cash value policy, buy term insurance as a death benefit if you plan to use the cash value for retirement.

Above all, insurance alternatives to pensions are not pensions. Think of it this way. A shoe is not a glove, but if the government made it very difficult to buy gloves, you might wear a shoe on your hand. All right, don't think of it that way.

The point is that the policy is being used for a secondary purpose for which it happens to be suited. That means that the state of your health, your age, and the mortality tables that are appropriate measures of death-benefit premiums will also dictate how much of your dollar is allocated for insurance as opposed to investing.

It also means that your future will be in the hands of the investment adviser of insurance companies. They are getting better all the time, but they are still outperformed by money managers and mutual fund managers.

AS WITH PENSIONS—CHECK SAFETY

Finally, as we asked about pensions: How safe is your insurance company? In 1990, A. M. Best, a company that rates insurance companies, reported that 46.3 percent of the assets of the top 125 insurance companies were invested in bonds. The top 125 account for 84.3 percent of the industry's $1.3 trillion in investments. Non-investment-grade bonds made up 3 percent; long-term and mortgage loans represented 76 percent. Therefore, junk bonds don't seem to be a serious problem leading to an insurance company's collapse, but real estate foreclosures bringing mortgage defaults could be. To help you judge insurance company safety, see Chapter 21.

Social, Yes; Security, No!

When I was sixty-five, it was a very good year. Provided I was born before 1943!

ADRIANE G. BERG

A disclaimer before we begin. I am a member of the board of the American Association of Baby Boomers, a not-for-profit corporation dedicated to lobbying for the rights of baby boomers (and getting us some nifty travel and other discounts too). Before I was elected to the board, the organization sued the United States government for misuse of Social Security funds. Even though I am not part of the suit, and even though I do not harbor hope of victory, I think the suit is legitimate. It is certainly raising our consciousness about the frailty of the Social Security system. Here's why.

Our Social Security system is supposed to take in more than it spends and keep the excess in a trust for future recipients (us).

Problem: The money is not kept in trust. It's in Treasury bills, sold to reduce our overall deficit. The government has always paid back the trust with interest, so far. But there is no guarantee that it will continue to do so. The ERISA laws that govern private pensions require an employer to segregate pension funds and to use them for no other purpose, least of all borrowing to pay other debts. An employer who did what our government is doing could go to jail under certain circumstances. The fact is that our Social Security trust fund contains only IOUs. If Social Security were made subject to ERISA laws, the case would be a winner.

Assuming the United States government makes good on its

IOUs (and to be fair, it always has), there are still problems. A big problem is us! We all are going to retire and call upon the system in unprecedented droves. To make matters worse, the ratio of workers contributing to the system to recipients of the system has declined from 42:1 in 1937 to 3:1 today. In response to this imbalance, the amount of yearly income subject to Social Security withholding has increased twenty times since the thirties. Further, in 1983 the government increased the percentage of Social Security taxes and slowed the distribution of future benefits.

These are the particulars of the system as they stand today:

You are fully insured if you have worked for forty quarters with paid-in coverage (these quarters need not be consecutive).

In 1992 the law changed to require a pay-in of 7.65 percent of your earnings up to $55,000 and 1.45 percent from $55,500 up to $130,200. Your employer must match that. If you are self-employed, you pay double.

When you file to receive benefits, the amount you get is a function of how long you have worked, when you stopped, and how much you have earned.

If you continue to work after receiving benefits you will give back $1 for every $2 you earn if you are under sixty-five, $1 for every $3 you earn if you are over sixty-five, and nothing if you are over seventy. There are yearly amounts you can earn before the payback is calculated: $7,440 per year before age sixty-five and $10,200 per year after age sixty-five.

Social Security is subject to federal income tax and, in some states, state income tax.

Analysts agree that the Social Security surplus will peak at $9 trillion somewhere between the year 2027 and 2030. Social Security will then be depleted within sixteen years. In recognition of this problem, the eligibility ages for Social Security have already been postponed on a sliding scale for baby boomers and their children. Starting with those born in 1943, eligibility age will rise from sixty-five up to sixty-seven, which will be the age for those born after 1960.

How to Use the Social Security System to
Make Up for Lost Time

Despite the restrictions of the Social Security system and the problems it faces, I believe that we can still count on it to provide some help in making up for lost time. It clearly cannot be relied on entirely. It is simply an additional source of retirement income for you to plug into the calculations found in Chapter 12 that tell you how much of a retirement shortfall you must take into account in making up for lost time. To make the most of the Social Security system, here are some suggestions:

Keep up with changes. Listen to the financial news. Locate your local Social Security office and get its annual rules publication.

Estimate your future benefits by filling out the Earnings and Benefit Estimate Statement for you and your spouse. Call 1-800-772-1213 to request forms from the Social Security Administration, or pick them up at your local Social Security office. File the requests several times. Vary the retirement age each time to get an estimate of benefits if you work after age sixty-five or retire early. It will take several weeks to get the estimate. While you are waiting, use 20 percent of your present before-tax salary as a rule of thumb to calculate your Social Security entitlement. Your financial planner also has precise information on your benefits and always takes Social Security into consideration when constructing a plan.

Check the government's figures of how much you have paid in over the years. If you have no records, start keeping them now.

If you have not gotten credit for forty quarters, try to get a job or start a business so you can pay in for full vesting. Despite all its problems, you still want to qualify for Social Security.

Consider taking benefits at age sixty-two, not sixty-five. Your estimate will show you that you will get about 20 percent less in benefits if you were born before 1960 and 30 percent less if you were born after 1960. But you will be receiving benefits three years longer. Therefore, if you anticipate living a good deal longer than twelve years after retirement, do not take early retirement. If longevity is not your strong suit, take early Social Security.

If you plan to work after age sixty-five, you can delay collecting Social Security. If you do this, the eventual annual benefit will increase between 1 and 8 percent, depending on how much you've paid in.

Let's say you were born in 1948 and needed to make up for lost time. Your full retirement age is sixty-six. You would receive an 8 percent yearly increase for each year you wait to start benefits after retirement age. If you wait until age seventy to retire, an extra four years, you get a total yearly increase of 32 percent. Working after seventy gives you no benefits, however.

It's pretty clear that with or without full benefits, we need to put more money in private pensions than ever before. If we never understood the intricacies of our private benefits and how to maximize them, we must do so now. Social Security is merely one line on a complex retirement planning form. It is not, by itself, a retirement plan.

Because so much of our savings will be devoted to our own retirement, we will need to employ special tactics to send our kids to college. Let's explore some.

COLLEGE PLANNING

Mother to Son:

Pick up your socks.

Son to Mother:

Pick up the tab.

ADRIANE G. BERG

GETTING A BEAD ON COLLEGE COSTS

Facing facts is the first step toward financing your kids' college education. The clearer you are about what it's really going to cost, the more likely you are to make the grade. The numbers are frightening: So far, tuition hikes are exceeding inflation by double each year. *Money* magazine reports that for 1993–94, a 7 percent rise is expected in private colleges' tuition and a 10 to 12 percent rise in public colleges' and universities' tuition.

While different reports give slightly different figures, here's what *Money* and *U.S. News & World Report* say are the average 1992 costs for a private college per year:

$10,017—tuition

$4,396—room and board

$508—books

$911—lab fees, dues, and other expenses

These costs go way down when the institution is a public college or a university:

$2,137—tuition

$3,351—room and board

$485—books

$1,147—lab fees, dues, and other expenses

If present-day costs are not overwhelming enough, the situation gets really scary when you add an increased cost factor for each year between now and your child's first year in college. For example, if your child is nine years old now, by the time he or she is college age, the tuition will be double what I've quoted from the magazines.

To learn the precise costs of the college in which you are interested, call the school's bursar's office. It will give present costs as well as make tentative projections. Also write to:

American Association of Community and Junior Colleges
One Dupont Circle, Suite 410
Washington, DC 20036

Association of Independent Colleges and Universities
122 C Street NW, Suite 750
Washington, DC 20001–2190

National Association of State Universities and Land Grant Colleges
One Dupont Circle, Suite 710
Washington, DC 20036

As you research the actual cost of college, you probably will not be happy with what you learn. The cost of college is taking a definite toll on the ability of the American middle class to get their children to college. In 1989, children with parents earning between $40,000 and $75,000 a year accounted for 31 percent of the students in top colleges. This is down 30 percent from 1978. The attrition continues.

Yet there are survival techniques for getting kids to college. And in order for us baby boomers to get our kids to college, we must pull out all the stops and use the whole bag of tricks, tools, and techniques.

FINANCIAL AID FROM COLLEGES

If you have no savings for college, and you are a member of the middle class, the present likelihood is that your child will not receive financial aid. Eligibility for financial aid is having your income just cover the cost of living that is dictated in the school's financial aid formula. If your income is higher than this, if there is money left over, you must spend it for education and financial aid is denied. The cost-of-living allowance is so low and out of sync with reality that few middle-class families qualify for substantial aid.

To enhance your chances of getting aid, here are some thoughts—some new, some old, some outrageous—to give your family an edge:

- Invest in assets that are not counted on aid applications. Get a few copies of financial aid forms from the colleges your child may attend. Most don't ask for a statement of pension plans, tax-deferred annuities, or life insurance cash-surrender values. These are the very investments you are likely to have made for retirement. Always save for your retirement first. You are expected to contribute 5 percent of your assets to pay tuition, whereas a whopping 35 percent of assets in your child's name must be contributed toward education costs. Yet another good reason to build your own assets first.

- Minimize your capital gains and income in the year you apply for aid. To the extent you are able, reduce your income by having your company pay salary in the form of benefits and pension contributions. College aid year is also the year to make cash payments for luxuries in order to reduce your assets. It is not the year to increase your income by selling appreciated assets.

- Sell an appreciated asset to pay for tuition. But first, transfer it to your child. If he or she sells it, the capital gain will be taxed at the child's own, lower rate.
- Be timely. Study the college's financial aid form (FAF) every year from the time your child reaches the age of fifteen. Take a look at the form provided by the Conference Report, House of Representatives, available from many colleges' financial offices. Also get a copy of the free application for federal student aid (available from your child's high school guidance office). Call two colleges of your choice and ask for their supplemental aid forms.

Speed and completeness of application make a world of difference in getting financial aid. A few years of dry runs will make you a pro in the actual year of application. This will also keep you in touch with changing eligibility rules and give you lead time to adjust finances accordingly. For example:

1. As of 1993, the financial aid form does not count the assets of families earning less than $50,000 a year that do not itemize deductions. Planning in advance, you can pay medical bills and make charitable contributions and other expenditures that favor itemizing. By the time the financial aid year rolls around, you could stop itemizing and take the standard deduction. Many of the income tax savings of itemization will already be yours.

2. In 1993, the federal government stopped counting home equity as an asset. By knowing this early, you might find it useful to use savings to pay off a mortgage and increase noncountable equity.

COLLEGE WORK-STUDY

There are two kinds of work-study situations for a student who needs money. The first is generally offered by most colleges and universities. The school makes a number of jobs available to needy students as part of their financial aid package so they can work a certain number of hours a week. In addition there are often jobs available for students who have not qualified for financial aid. Students can apply for these jobs at the college financial aid office.

The second work-study program, cooperative education, is available only at certain colleges which offer students the opportunity to earn while they learn. That is, they alternate periods of work with periods of study. Thus, students are able to help finance their own education, with the college assisting them in finding work in their field of interest. Information about these cooperative programs can be obtained from the National Commission for Cooperative Education, 360 Huntington Avenue, Boston, MA 02115.

TAKE ADVANTAGE OF UNCLE SAM

STAFFORD LOANS

When your child reaches the age of fifteen, start to keep up with federal aid and federal loan programs. As of now, about half of all aid comes from the Stafford Loan program. The payback period on these loans does not start until six months after the student leaves school. At present, the interest rate is 6.94 percent, adjusted every July to match the ninety-one-day Treasury bill of the prior June. The Stafford PLUS program permits parents to borrow up to $4,000 a year at favorable rates.

Stafford loans are now available to all students, regardless of financial aid qualification. For those who do not meet the need qualifications, however, the payback period begins immediately upon securing the loan, not after graduation.

BASIC GRANTS

Another major program offered by the federal government is the Basic Grant program. Its grants may be used at any approved postsecondary educational institution, including a college, technical institute, or vocational school. Grants are awarded on the basis of financial need, not academic achievement. If a student is admitted to an approved institution, and if the family's income meets income guidelines, the student will receive a grant. The guidelines were recently revised to include middle-class families.

After family size, assets, and expenses are taken into consideration, a family with an income in the $25,000 range may qualify for government aid. You should apply for the Basic Grant even though you may think you're not eligible. All you need to do is check the "Basic Grants" box on the Parent's Confidential (Financial) Statement form of the College Scholarship Service. Many colleges use this form in evaluating financial need. You may also apply directly.

Forms for Basic Grants are available from your child's high school guidance office, or from Basic Grants, P.O. Box 84, Washington, DC 20044. (When requesting the forms, also ask for the free booklet *Meeting College Costs*.) If you are found eligible for a grant, the amount of money you receive will be based on family income and the tuition of the schools to which your child is applying.

It is wise to send in your application early. Forms for Basic Grants are not available until January. You should apply as soon as you receive your forms—an early application will receive an early response.

SUPPLEMENTAL EDUCATIONAL OPPORTUNITY GRANTS

If a family's income is below $6,000, a Supplemental Educational Opportunity Grant (SEOG) may be available. An SEOG is worth double its face amount, since the school must match it with other financial aid funds. These are administered through the college financial aid office. To apply, find out the procedure from the financial aid officer at the college your child plans to attend. Different colleges are allocated different amounts that they can offer in aid under the SEOG federal program.

The student applying for an SEOG must be a citizen or permanent resident of the United States and must be enrolled at least half time in a college accredited by the U.S. Office of Education.

NATIONAL MERIT SCHOLARSHIPS

Toward the end of a student's high school years, you will hear a great deal about National Merit Scholarships. These are available even to students who plan to attend state and local institutions.

The scholarships are awarded mainly on the results of a competitive examination given by the federal government in the student's junior year. Service to the school, recommendation by the school principal, and financial need are also considered.

The government awards a thousand scholarships of $1,000 each, and another three thousand scholarships ranging from $250 to $1,500.

The National Merit Scholarships test is administered routinely. For additional information, simply inquire at your child's high school guidance office.

STATE LOANS

Many states have their own loan programs. Guaranteed Student Loans are available for up to $2,500 per year for undergraduates, $5,000 per year for graduate students. Both now have an 8 percent interest rate and repayment doesn't begin until six months after graduation. They shine in comparison to the 14.75 percent interest on a personal loan. Applications are available through banks and are submitted to the school, whose financial officer makes the decision.

For graduate students, an Auxiliary Loans Program (with 12

percent interest and the payback period beginning six months after graduation) is available in many states.

MILITARY SCHOLARSHIPS

An Army Reserve Officers Training Corps (ROTC) scholarship can provide as much as $3,000 over four years. To qualify, students must be at least seventeen years old, high school graduates, and citizens of the United States. Although ROTC is usually a four-year program, scholarships for two-year programs are available for junior and community college students. Scholarships also are available for those who agree to enlist after college for a period of four years of active and two years of reserve duty. With these, the military pays for full tuition, books, college fees, and a small stipend for pocket money.

ROTC scholarships are based on merit. Students must score well on scholastic aptitude tests, show leadership ability in extra-curricular and school activities, and do well in personal interviews. Application forms may be requested from April 1 of the student's junior year through November 15, and from January 15 to April 15 of his or her senior year. Write to Army ROTC Scholarships, P.O. Box 12703, Philadelphia, PA 19134. If your child is already enlisted, write to Army ROTC Scholarships, Fort Monroe, VA 23651.

Other branches of the military also have extensive scholarship programs for both four- and two-year colleges. The programs differ in the age by which the student must complete his or her college term.

Many tuition-assisted programs are available if your child is already in the armed services. In fact, most advertisements seeking to expand our voluntary army appeal to young people on the basis of the educational opportunities available.

The child or spouse of a veteran who died or was seriously disabled because of military service may be entitled to an education benefit. For more information, write or call the nearest Veterans Administration Office (listed under U.S. Government in the phone book).

Loans and grants are also available to children of parents in the military. For a list, send $2 to the American Legion National Emblem Sales Department, P.O. Box 1055, Indianapolis, IN 46206, and ask for the booklet *Need a Lift?*

Design Your Own Package of Loans, Grants, and Scholarships

The likelihood is that you will get your children to college with a combination of loans, grants, private money, and scholarships. *Staying on top of all the help that is available is your best approach for making up for lost time.*

While there is no guarantee that all the resources listed in this section will be available when you need them, or on the same terms, they are the current leaders in the field of making up for lost time where college is concerned.

Knight tuition payment plan. Knight pays the college; you pay Knight over a five- to ten-year period, with interest. Call 1-800-225-6783.

Nellie Maes. These are loans that can be secured with the equity in your home to make the interest tax-deductible. Call 1-800-363-9308.

Education Resource Institute. Just one of many commercial lenders that give loans to be repaid after graduation. Call 1-800-255-8347. (*Note:* Credit checks are required with all commercial loans. There are new commercial lenders appearing every day. Your high school and college loan officers will give you a list.)

PLUS and SLS loans. These are federal loan programs for parents and graduate students. They lend at lower interest rates, but they lend less money than do the commercial lenders. Call 1-800-562-6872.

Prepaid tuition plans. If you can select your college early enough, you can enter into a prepaid plan that freezes the cost of college to a specific amount below the inflationary projection. If your child does not enter college or is not accepted, your money is returned, minus an administrative fee. You get prorated refunds if your child drops out or fails in later years. Check with your dream colleges. It's a good program for disciplined savers, or for the very undisciplined who need a structure in which to operate. However, Uncle Sam may tax the amount of college tuition you save in this program as if it were income. If you enter into one of these programs, get all details first. To find out about them, call the bursar of the colleges that interest you.

Private scholarships. These are few and far between. But if you want to try for them, start early. Your child usually must maintain a B or better average, get good college test scores, and be outstanding in some way, be it in music, athletics, or in another pursuit.

Scholarship computer programs that search out little-known sources are usually a waste of time because they use computerized lists of scholarships that really are not unknown and are often overapplied. When they do turn up new sources, these sources often contribute pennies. The ABC'S of Academic Scholarships, Octameron Associates, P.O. Box 2748, Alexandria, VA 22301, lists many small scholarships available from schools. Check all the organizations you belong to, and even your employer, to see if small grants and awards are available.

Unions have funds that are usually granted on merit to members' children. Many companies also give merit awards—sometimes big ones—to students entering particular fields. Ask about these at your union or company benefits office.

Numerous scholarships are awarded by the American Legion. Write to American Legion National Emblem Sales Department, P.O. Box 1055, Indianapolis, IN 46206.

Most states have special education programs for the handicapped. Ask the college financial aid office, or write to your state's division of vocational rehabilitation.

Also available are ethnic scholarships, such as those from

the United Negro College Fund, 500 East Sixty-second Street, New York, NY 10021.

The Boy Scouts, Girl Scouts, private foundations, 4-H Clubs, National Honor|Society, civic groups, trade associations, fraternities| and sororities—these| are just a sampling of some other sources of scholarship money.

INVESTOR'S STRATEGIES

If you can afford to save for your children's education, there is no mystery as to how to invest. As with long-term retirement planning, it is stocks that get you where you want to be. If you have only a few years in which to invest, however, the risk associated with stocks may be too great, and fixed-income investments are more secure and targeted.

In short, your college investment program simply parallels our Three-Tier system. If your child is within five years of college, Tier-One investments that give a predictable return at a given time are your choice. A Tier-One zero-coupon bond, Treasury, municipal, or high-quality corporate bond, all work. Better yet, diversify among all three. Unless you can make a large contribution, you may not meet your entire goal, but your contribution will be risk-free and quantifiable.

If your child is within five to seven years of starting college, you can add some growth potential with a Tier-Two mutual fund investing in stocks. Let's say you have $10,000 to invest for six years. Buy a zero-coupon bond that will return the $10,000 at the time of entry. Let's say this costs you $7,000. Invest the other $3,000 in a growth mutual fund.

If your child has more than seven years until college, you can use all Tier-Two growth investments. A combination of growth mutual funds, domestic and international, together with a few blue-chip stocks may not be sexy, but over time it has proven to give the best results.

If your child is very small, you can use a variety of what I call "plain vanilla" index funds that invest with the stock market indexes. These are no brainers, and they accumulate nicely over time.

Special Note: If you invest for college using zero-coupon bonds or another Tier-One investment with a maturity date, be sure that a good percentage of the investment matures before your child's first year in college. Often financial aid is less available in the first year. In addition, loans such as Stafford Loans start small and increase every year. Also, if your child does well the first year, the college may be more willing to offer a grant or a scholarship, for the next year(s). Be sure you've got that first year covered.

SERIES EE BONDS

EE bonds are federal bonds. If they are bought after you are twenty-four years old and are held in your own or in your spouse's name, they will be federally tax-free if used to pay tuition. However, in order to get the federal tax exemption, you must meet an income test. At present, a couple earning up to $60,000 a year qualifies. Series EE bond rates vary but cannot dip below a percentage fixed when you buy. So, at today's rate, if your child is ten years old, you can accumulate $12,051.44 if you contribute $100.00 a month until your child reaches college age.

BE TAX WISE

To decide in whose name investments should be made, you must understand the "Kiddie Tax." Before the age of fourteen, your child is taxed at the same rate as your marginal tax bracket for money earned from investing. However, the first $600 of unearned income is tax-free; the second $600 of unearned income is taxed at the child's own rate. So, at least enough to generate $1,200 a year can be invested in the child's name. Additional money invested for college until your child is age fourteen might otherwise be invested in your name. The tax will be at your rate, you will keep control of the money, and you will have more to invest in mutual funds and perhaps get a commission break.

When the child is fourteen, the child's tax bracket changes. He or she gets her own bracket—presumably one that's lower than yours. You can now put money as a gift in the child's name. If, however, the child has a shot at a grant, leave the money in your name alone. If you have a poor credit rating and would not be eligible for parent loans, keep all money in your name to give your child a shot at any of the loans I've mentioned in this chapter.

BE RADICAL

Have your child go to a two-year college first and make fabulous grades. Two-year colleges are inexpensive and not difficult to get into. Graduation will earn your child lots of credits toward a four-year degree. If your child does well, he or she can then apply to a four-year school, perhaps entering as a junior.

RETHINK COLLEGE TIMING

At present, a twenty-four-year-old who is married, who is a veteran, or who has dependent children is considered independent from his or her parents. The grants I've just discussed become far more available to the independent student.

Most of us were raised to see virtue in going immediately from high school to college. The Europeans, in contrast, believe in a hiatus to travel the world, get work experience, or find one's true calling. A term of work or serving in the armed services before college can contribute maturity and savings, as well as greater grant possibilities. It's true, your child may not graduate until he is thirty, but his path may be clear. He may be better off than we were, graduating at twenty-two but not finding our way until forty.

Furthermore, the older student can get life experience credits in many schools, reducing the overall cost of college.

How Families Who Work Together Can Make Up for Lost Time

Honor thy father and thy mother. And a little tax planning couldn't hurt either.

ADRIANE G. BERG

I give about five seminars a month on family finances, most of which are attended by two generations of students. This chapter answers the most important intergenerational planning questions asked in the seminars through the years. It will give you the practical knowledge you need so the whole family can work together to preserve family wealth.

Q: What is the first step to preserving family wealth?

A: *Having the right power of attorney.*

Power of attorney is a wealth protection device that is absolutely essential to your family. It is a simple document that authorizes the person of your choice to handle your investments, make gifts, transfer assets (and anything else you want to list) on your behalf. Parents often name each other as each's attorney. Then you or one of your siblings is named as the successor, in case a parent can't serve.

Power of attorney should be "durable." That means that even if your parent is legally incompetent to make decisions, the power allows the attorney in fact (you, your other parent, your sibling) to act in your parent's stead without an expensive court conservatorship proceeding.

Even though they seem self-explanatory, durability clauses are relatively new. If your parents signed an old version of power of attorney, its provisions are not protected in the event of Alzheimer's or other mentally degenerative diseases. The old version expires upon incompetency—just when you need it most.

Your parent may want to look into setting up a "standby" power of attorney. This becomes valid only at incompetency. The elder keeps all the control while able to handle his or her own finances.

Q: How can I talk to my parents about my inheritance?

A: *Lead off with a discussion of taxes, insurance, and the grandchildren.*

While there is no comfortable way to ask directly about parental intentions regarding your inheritance, there are a number of ways to discuss related topics that can help to save the family fortune. Invoking Uncle Sam is your best bet in getting your parents' attention focused on estate planning.

At present, up to 55 percent of an estate over $600,000 is subject to federal taxation. Add state estate taxes, and the percentage can soar up to 82 percent. Attorney's fees and probate costs can take another 6 percent, depending on the size and complexity of the estate.

Every year there is a new bill in Congress that opts to decrease the $600,000 exclusion. The numbers sound high, and most middle-class families do not see their assets threatened. They are wrong. If your parents' house appreciated a great deal in the real estate boom of the eighties, your family will lose a lot if they fail to plan for estate taxes. If the mortality tables are correct, longevity alone will bring the average taxpayer well above the $600,000 threshold, as a lifetime of savings accumulates with compound interest.

This is why you must talk about your parents' assets, if not for your benefit, then for the benefit of your children and your parents. Do not broach the subject directly. It can be painful and may cause suspicion in the most loving and trusting of parents. I know a lovely woman of seventy-eight who worried herself into a heart attack because her children asked about their inheritance. She was convinced it meant she had cancer.

Instead, talk law and taxes. Explore how to avoid probate with a trust, or how to save taxes by transferring assets. In the course of these discussions, parents can reveal the extent of their estate without feeling that they are relinquishing control. Most parents want their children to get the most money possible. If there is a way to plan properly, they are usually very receptive to hearing about it.

If all else fails, you at least have to know where their assets are located. If your parents become incompetent or die, secret assets do nobody any good.

To facilitate matters, I have created an audiotape series called *Saving the Family Fortune* which includes a form to give your parents. They can fill it out and leave it in a place known to you. In this way, you have access to the knowledge when you need it, but not so early that they become uncomfortable. (Call 1-800-934-2211 for more information about *Saving the Family Fortune*.)

Q: How can I talk to my parents about borrowing money from them?

A: *Keep it strictly business.*

These days, you may need a loan for a new business, a new residence, or to tide you over while you look for a job. If your credit is poor, the family may be your best resource. There are right ways and wrong ways to borrow money from parents. The wrong way is to keep the arrangement vague, never articulating whether it is a loan or a gift, or when repayment is due. The anxiety over the unspoken issues can ruin the relationship.

The right way is to first be clear whether or not a gift is intended. If it is, and you have a sibling, tell your parents that you will expect that the gift be deemed an "advance against inheritance." This can be spelled out in your parents' will. It means that you are getting some of the inheritance early, and that this is not an additional gift. Some parents want to give or leave more to one child. If so, discuss how the gift will be regarded by your sibling and include him or her in the plan if appropriate.

If the transfer of assets is a loan, do it legally. Be sure that a note and/or a mortgage or other collateral is provided. Pay your parents interest. In fact, if you get an interest-free loan, the Internal Revenue Service may regard it as either a gift or as reportable income and tax it accordingly.

As with any creditor, be realistic. Don't promise to repay if repayment is a pipe dream. Above all, don't ask or permit parents to borrow against their home or life savings for you. If their well-being is put in jeopardy, and if things do not work out for you, the whole family will go under.

Q: In whose name should gifts to my children from my parents and from me be held?

A: *It depends on the age of your child.*

1. Keep an amount that will generate up to $1,200 per year in the name of each minor in a Uniform Gifts to Minors Act account with you as custodian. Any bank, brokerage house, or mutual fund can set one up (see Chapter 18 to learn about the tax benefits of doing this).

2. Keep all other sums in your own name, invested in the way that is best for you.

3. When children reach the age of fourteen, leave whatever money is saved for them in your name if you think they may be entitled to financial aid for college. If not, transfer money you have saved for them to their names as a gift, using a Uniform Gift to Minors Act account (UGMA) or a Uniform Transfers to Minors Act account (UTMA).

4. If amounts are substantial, create a trust for the minor with specific distribution requirements, i.e., money for school, money to be provided when he or she reaches a certain age, money to start a business. (You may transfer up to $10,000 per year per child, or $20,000 from both parents).

Q: What are an UTMA and an UGMA?

A: *They are the most popular types of custodial accounts.*

An UTMA, available in thirty states, and an UGMA, available in virtually all states, are accounts which are similar except that in an UGMA gifts can be only insurance policies, bank deposits, mutual funds, and securities, whereas all types of property as gifts are allowed in an UTMA. These are their positive and negative features.

Pros

1. The income from investments held in an UGMA is taxed at the lower income tax rate of the child if the child is fourteen or older (it's taxed at your bracket for those under fourteen).
2. The use of the money (and the income from it) can be controlled by the donor throughout the minority of the child; this includes using it for the health and welfare of the child.
3. The gift will automatically go to the child at the age of twenty-one.

Cons

1. The gift is irrevocable: Once given it cannot be taken back.
2. If the child should die before age twenty-one, the money will be taxed in his or her estate.
3. If the donor should die before the child reaches the age of twenty-one, the money will be taxed in the donor's estate.

Forms for establishing UGMAs and UTMAs are available from your bank, brokerage house, or mutual fund.

Q: How should my parents invest money they want to gift to my kids?

A: *Use the Three-Tier system.*

The best investments for kids are found on page 181 of this book. Your parents should follow the same pattern I suggest for you. Invest in equity mutual funds until your children are over the age of fourteen. Then ease into balanced funds that contain stocks and bonds. If the interest rates are good and if your children are within five years of college age, go for zero-coupon bonds (see page 77). But, remember, your parents may be very conservative. They may be confident only about bank deposits, U.S. Treasuries, or EE bonds. So be it. Let them make those investments and be happy they are willing to give.

Q: All my investment professionals dislike joint accounts. Yet my parents put a lot of their money in such accounts. What is a joint account and are joint accounts okay?

A: *A joint account is a simple way to title the ownership of assets to avoid probate and to make gifts. I believe it to be a dangerous way as well.*

Two kinds of gifts can be set up jointly: joint tenancy and tenants in common. A joint tenancy creates ownership of the entire sum by both parties. Both parents and child own the whole gift. Neither can sell or otherwise transfer his or her half without the participation of the other. Neither owner may use the property as collateral without the other's knowledge and consent. If you create a joint tenancy with a child or grandchild and the child dies, the amount will be fully inherited by you, the survivor; if you die first, the amount is fully inherited by the child.

By contrast, in a tenants-in-common arrangement, each tenant owns a half interest in the property. If one dies, his or her heirs, not the surviving half owner, inherits.

There are a variety of ways to set up joint ownership:

1. A joint bank account can be opened in your name and your child's (or another's) name by your parent. A gift is considered to have been made (and a gift tax incurred) when either party withdraws money. No tax is incurred if the amount gifted is less than $10,000 a year.

2. A U.S. bond in two names can be purchased. The purchaser may cash in the bond tax-free; the other party would pay a gift tax upon cashing in the bond.

3. Joint stock may be purchased. Naming a joint owner establishes that a gift has been made.

4. Real estate may be put in another person's name. A gift is considered to have been made when the new deed is issued.

JOINT OWNERSHIP IS A TRICKY BUSINESS

If a parent and child are joint owners and one of them dies, the amount of holdings added to the decedent's estate is determined by who purchased and contributed to the holdings. (It may be possible for all the holdings to be considered part of the estate of the first to die.)

There is also some confusion as to the proper method of taxing joint accounts when they earn income or capital gains. At least one tax court has held that interest earned on joint tenancies is taxable to the owners in proportion to their contribution. Another court has held that the contributions were immaterial and that the taxes are to be placed on an equal basis.

Another point to consider is the use of Social Security numbers in opening joint accounts. Frequently, a lower-tax-paying grandmother will, without informing her children or grandchildren, set up a joint account. The interest from that account is money that she expects to declare and pay taxes on at her lower bracket and rate. If the Social Security number of the child is listed first, however, the government may consider the funds to be those of the child. If the unsuspecting adult fails to report income earned on the asset, an audit may result.

Using Joint and In-Trust-For Accounts to Avoid Probate

Many seniors open joint, in-trust-for, or payable-on-death accounts in order to avoid probate and save the cost of making a will. While this works, what seniors don't realize is that a credit, marital, or tax problem affecting the beneficiary or joint owner also affects the asset. A creditor, spouse, or the IRS can attach the asset even before the senior dies. This may be the senior's life nest egg, and such accounts put those funds in jeopardy.

Sometimes seniors believe that these accounts protect the assets from taxation or qualify them from Medicaid. Not true. The funds are counted as 100 percent their own unless the joint owner can prove that he or she personally contributed funds.

The current popularity of these accounts stems from the secretiveness many seniors feel about their inheritance plans. By keeping the passbook and not telling the beneficiary about the account, a senior hopes to avoid pressure from the heir regarding the money. *The Result: Thousands of dollars in middle-class inheritance are lost each year, because heirs have no knowledge of the location of their parents' assets.*

Please talk to your parents about the dangers of these accounts. Discuss a revocable trust, which avoids probate and leaves them in complete control of their money, or a simple will instead.

Q: I have heard of using revocable trusts to avoid probate. Can you explain them?

A: *A revocable trust is one of the best devices for keeping financial control within the family and out of the courts. Here's why:*

1. To create a living trust, your parents must sign a document that names them trustee and controller of the trust. In this way they are still in charge of their own money. When they die or become infirm, you take over as successor trustee. You distribute the money in accordance with their wishes, free of probate or conservatorship. In my book *Warning: Dying May Be Hazardous to Your Wealth* (Hawthorne, NJ: Career Press, 1993), you can learn the pros and cons. Such trusts cost from $900 to $2,500 to set up.

2. If your parents want you to have the money right now, they should make an outright gift. If the gift exceeds $10,000, a gift tax may have to be paid. For more information, see the Bibliography.

3. To save estate taxes, parents can hold money in an irrevocable trust. They cannot control the investments, but they can receive income for life and save estate taxes (see the Bibliography).

Q: How can I build the biggest inheritance for myself and my children?

A: *Consider paying the premiums on a joint-and-survivor policy with your parents as the measuring lives.*

A policy called "second-to-die" or "joint-and-survivor" can create the maximum legacy for you and your children. These policies are available only to husbands and wives or business partners. The death benefit is paid when both parties die.

Because of the joint underwriting and mortality table, this insurance is very economical and can be used to create a large estate. If your parents are healthy and in their sixties, such policies can be paid for by you, to create your own inheritance. You may want to buy one of your own for your children's inheritance.

Q: My parents need financial assistance. How can I help them?

A: Contact the resources listed below.

If your parents need help, encourage them to seek aid. Often they are ashamed and equate aid to seniors with welfare or public assistance. The fact is, our government has sensitively separated these two types of entitlements. You can assure your parents and yourself that they are not on the welfare rolls. They can apply for

Supplementary Security Income (SSI), available from their Social Security Office.

Medicaid, which provides extensive medical coverage. Apply at their state's Department of Social Services.

Food Stamps. Contact their state's Department of Social Services.

Senior Housing Assistance. Check with their state's Department of Social Services.

Hill-Burton Programs, which provide limited free hospital care if your parents are not eligible for Medicaid. Check with their region's Department of Health and Human Services.

To help you negotiate the maze of the many programs available for seniors, read the books suggested in the Bibliography and keep in touch with your state's Department of the Aging.

Q: What is the best way to plan for my parents' potential need for long-term health care?

A: Understanding Medicaid qualifications and asset transfer are all part of the picture.

Our parents are rightly sensitive to the relinquishment of asset control. Rather than viewing it as an expected financial-planning strategy, they see it as a symbol of their old age. On the other hand, most seniors fear that their hard-earned assets will disappear in a matter of months if they need long-term nursing home care unless they transfer their assets to a family member.

Medicare is a government health care program available to all seniors regardless of wealth, but it does not pay for the nonskilled care required for conditions and diseases of longevity like dementia, senility, Alzheimer's, Parkinson's, and blindness.

Medicaid, a means-tested program meant to be available only to the impoverished, does pay for long-term-care costs. Much like the college tuition trap that the middle class faces, when nursing home or in-house extended care is needed, we are too poor to pay for private help and too rich to qualify for government aid. This has led many seniors to transfer assets in order to impoverish themselves for Medicaid eligibility.

In some states (New York, Connecticut, Pennsylvania, and more to come) Medicaid is available up front for those with substantial assets (i.e., $250,000), provided they have a qualifying long-term health care insurance policy. If your state has a similar allowance, meet with an insurance agent to help your parents select a policy.

These policies are much improved lately and can be designed for the extent, length, and type of service you require. The state Department of Social Services or the equivalent in your area will give you the rules for judging whether a policy qualifies to meet the Medicaid eligibility rules.

If none of these options work for your parents, assets may have to be transferred. And an elderlaw specialist can counsel them. They may want to transfer their assets outright or put them in trust. Either way, they are relinquishing control in order to protect your inheritance from the costs of long-term care.

At present, such transfers must be made within thirty-six months of applying for aid, or the transferred amounts will still be counted as available assets. That means that a wise program of timed transfers is in order. Keep money in your parents' name so at least when you apply for entry to a home they can afford to pay for at least thirty-six months. This can be coupled with an insurance policy to further conserve the family fortune.

It is my hope that by the time this book goes to press a new national health care program that realizes the cost of our longevity will come to our rescue. If not, consult one of the many fine professionals who specializes in transfer-of-asset planning.

However, in order to make wise decisions in this area, educate yourself first. The quickest road is to pick up

Adriane G. Berg, *Warning: Dying May Be Hazardous to Your Wealth* (Hawthorne, NJ: Career Press, 1993) (available in bookstores).

———, *Saving the Family Fortune* (audiotape series; call 1-800-934-2211).

Harley Gordon, *How to Protect Your Life Savings from Catastrophic Illness and Nursing Homes* (Boston: Financial Planning Institute, 1990) (available in bookstores).

Alice M. Rivlin and Joshua M. Wiener, *Caring for the Disabled Elderly* (Washington, DC: The Brookings Institution, 1988) (available through the publisher).

PART V

OLD WINE IN NEW BOTTLES: MAKING UP FOR LOST TIME WITH CREDIT AND DEBT, INSURANCE, AND REAL ESTATE

CREDIT: "THE DEVIL WITH THE

RED DRESS ON"

Sometimes credit is good to use, but sometimes you can get into trouble. Being able to tell the difference is very important.

ARTHUR BERG BOCHNER (AGE 11),
The Totally Awesome Money Book for Kids (and Their Parents)

Credit is an opportunity: It is the right to borrow money. Once you take advantage of that opportunity, you have turned it into an obligation called "debt." My point is not to give you a simple definition. The likelihood is that you know all too well the meaning of credit and debt. My objective is to change the way you think about credit forever.

There is no greater barrier to making up for lost time than the obligation to pay past debts. I'm still paying for debt incurred in 1988 as a result of my failed real estate investments. I probably will continue to pay all my life. A psychic once told me that he thought I had made a money mistake in a past life that I am paying off in this one.

While the theory is interesting, the fact is that middle-class Americans have a perverted credit culture that is a threat to physical well-being and peace of mind. In order to make up for lost time, we not only must correct our past credit record, we must correct our future credit use as well.

There are three types of credit that affect our lives: (1) credit for consumables, (2) credit for investments, and (3) credit to start a business, overcome a job loss, go to school, or finance other life events.

Each of these is different in purpose, but all are dreadfully overused, often to the point of disaster. Our whole credit system tells us that we deserve to indulge in the present, even at the expense of the future. If we have an unused line of credit, to some of us it feels like money burning a hole in our pocket. But credit is not money. It is a way of buying money at a very high price.

THE COST OF CREDIT

What do you pay for your money? If you earn money, you are paying with your time. The higher your earnings per hour, the less you pay. When comparing jobs, we always consider the salaries offered.

When we borrow money, however, we don't fully consider what it costs us. Accepting credit causes us to pay for our borrowed money in interest costs. If interest rates are low, it may be a good deal. If they are high, borrowing can be a disaster.

Moral: Do not ask whether you can afford the monthly payments. Instead, ask whether the item you plan to buy is worth the total price, including financing. You'll use a lot less credit that way.

BECOME CONSUMER DEBT-FREE

In my private struggle with credit, debt, and creditors, I learned a lot about the emotional, procedural, and legal aspects of credit and debt. As a result, today I am practically a credit "teetotaler." Though I am not dogmatic about it since a good credit record is an important asset. It's okay to use credit carefully, but if you can't do that, it's much better not to use credit at all.

In 1987 I cut up my credit cards on the air during one of my WMCA broadcasts. I joked that my purse groaned and would miss the company. I have never sought a new card. Prior to cutting them up, my family charged as much as $6,000 per *month* on our cards! Yet at no time have I ever missed the use of the cards or felt deprived. Without any budget effort, my guess is that we saved $30,000 a year by eliminating the use of our credit cards. We were not in credit card debt. We paid most of the bill each month, but we were using up our future by saving nothing in the present.

I know that because my income and expenses were high my personal numbers may not relate to your lifestyle. But I also know that they are not so different proportionately for most of you. During my credit-free half decade, I learned a lot about the emotions surrounding the use of credit. Maybe some of my revelations will help you stop spending your future and start making up for lost time.

ADRIANE BERG'S PROFOUND PUNCH LINES ON CONSUMER CREDIT

Consumer Credit Gives You a False Sense of Power.

At the cash register, the customer is king. No matter how low your self-esteem, you never get rejected if you are spending money. Credit lets you spend at will. You often buy things that may have no meaning within five minutes after purchase. It's the transaction, the shopping, that is the reward, not the material thing itself. True shopaholics don't even bother to open the package once they get home.

Consumer Credit Is Billed as a Measure of Success.

All the ads for credit cards show well-turned-out people, exuding an aura of financial success. Credit cards even come in precious-metal colors like gold and platinum. The cardholder is portrayed in ads as a richer, worthier, special person. Having a big credit line and using it for consumables is plugged as a measure of personal success. If you decide to curtail your use of credit, you must protect yourself from loss of self-esteem.

When You First Leave Home Without Your Card, You May Feel Scared.

A credit card is useful in case of a rare emergency, i.e., your tire blows out and you don't have the cash for an immediate replacement. The legitimate convenience of the card makes a good excuse for carrying one. If you are disciplined enough to pass up the expensive lunch or the once-in-a-lifetime sale, carry the card. But don't let the occasional convenience be your excuse for continued use of consumer credit.

The Spirit Eventually Cleanses Itself of Material Waste, Just as the Body Cleanses Itself of Toxic Waste.

After five years without a card, I could carry one for a year and never use it. I'm amazed at all the things I don't want now that I have disciplined myself not to buy on impulse. Very rarely have I gone back to buy something I liked and been short of cash or checks. Most of the time I forget all about the thing, not cluttering my closet or depleting my bankbook. It takes no effort and causes no deprivation. When I do go back and buy, it's something I really want and use with gusto.

Not Using a Card Makes You Feel a Little Weird.

American commerce is not accustomed to cash. I have been told by salespeople that the cash register is closed because it's dangerous to open it, but that I could make the purchase with my credit card. I travel almost every week, usually to promote my books or speak. I must arrange in advance for a rental car with a $200 deposit. I often have to prepay my hotel bill. So what? Having to pay by cash or check often results in a better focus on travel plans.

A NOBLE EXPERIMENT REGARDING CONSUMER CREDIT

Take a look at your credit card expenditures. If you cut out the unnecessaries, how much could you contribute yearly to a Tier-

Two mutual fund? Look at the chart on page 58 to calculate how much that would add up to in five years.

Most employed people truly believe they cannot save, yet they charge many unimportant items on their card. If you are one of them, you can speed up your MUFLT efforts by making investing just as easy as charging. Pick any mutual fund, even a simple index fund. Then watch your card purchases for two months. It is likely that a pattern of unnecessary spending will emerge. Cut it out. Authorize your bank to deposit the saved amount each month in the fund. All it takes is a one-time authorization to the fund. They will send you a form. I'll bet that you will never miss the stuff and that you will appreciate the speed at which your future is growing.

CREDIT AND PROCEDURE: OF CREDIT COUNSELORS, COLLECTORS, AND CREDIT REPAIR

Making up for lost time is impossible if you are in over your head in consumer debt with your stomach in knots over monthly bills. Your first step in making up for lost time must be to get your day-to-day expenses under control. Even if you need a debt payback program, it is essential to start as soon as possible.

While you are taking some of the steps outlined in this chapter, don't despair. Most of us have gone through a bad patch at one time or another. One of my divorced clients had her electricity turned off when her husband refused to pay the bills, which she had thought were being paid all along. Despite the pain of the divorce itself, she never felt suicidal until that time. I realize that there is much shame and anxiety associated with debt, but eventually it all works out. I hope you will take comfort in knowing that you are not alone.

If consumer debt becomes overwhelming to you and prevents the start of a MUFLT Three-Tier program, here are the steps you should take.

SEE A COUNSELOR AT CONSUMER CREDIT COUNSELING (CCC)

Years ago I taught a course at the New School for Social Research for paralegals-in-training. As part of their work, they volunteered to help provide credit counseling at the New York Budget and Credit Counseling Services (BUCCS), the flagship local arm of a national nonprofit organization called Consumer Credit Counseling (CCC). It was run then, as it is now, by renowned consumer advocate Luther Gatling. If this local organization is any example, then CCC is the most nurturing and trustworthy place to solve your credit problems.

The CCC centers will juggle the creditors' demands until an agreement on payback over a several-year period is achieved. Each branch is aware that part of your needs is to make up for lost time, and its counselors will include, as part of a realistic program, some immediate savings strategies for you and your family. Once a program is arranged, you will make payments to CCC, shielding you from the anxiety of direct contact with creditors. To contact one of CCC's 580 offices, nationwide, call 1-800-338-2227.

IF YOU ARE A PARAGON OF EMOTIONAL STABILITY, HANDLE YOUR OWN PAYBACK PROGRAM

In his books and newsletters, John Ventura, a legal and consumer expert on credit repair and bankruptcy, outlines a program of dealing with creditors yourself. Mr. Ventura is a frequent and valued guest on my radio shows. I think of him as an optimist. Most people are afraid of creditors and cannot withstand the stress of working out a plan. They often promise too much and can't deliver. A broken settlement is worse than the initial debt. If you have nerves of steel, follow the Ventura system as outlined in *Fresh Start* (Chicago: Dearborn, 1992).

In addition, if you are serious about handling your own payback system, read books on negotiation, such as Roger Fisher and William Wry, *Getting to Yes: Negotiating Agreement Without Giving In*

(Cambridge, MA: Harvard Negotiation Project, Penguin, 1991). It's a classic in the field. Essentially, you must remove your focus from the fact that you are dealing for yourself and instead must cultivate an objective attitude. The negotiation must be treated as business and left on the doorstep when you go home at night. If you can learn to be a fair and effective negotiator in solving your own credit problems, you will learn a skill worth its weight in gold—a skill that, although born of adversity, will change your life; perhaps even bring you to a whole new career.

KNOW YOUR RIGHTS

Whether you use a counselor or do your own negotiation, you must negotiate from strength (even though you feel weak). Here are some tips that can help.

- The Federal Fair Debt Collection Practices Act give you several rights. Collectors cannot harass you; they may not call you at odd hours or at work. The Federal Trade Commission enforces these rules, and you are given thirty days in which to correct an incorrect demand. You can get a copy of the act through a regional office or by contacting the Federal Trade Commission, Sixth and Pennsylvania Avenue NW, Washington, DC 20580, or calling 202-326-2222.
- Keep records of all your conversations with creditors and collectors. If they don't back off, tell them you are recording your conversation each time, and do it. Use common sense, however. Don't anger a cooperative creditor by putting him on the hot seat.
- If you do make a deal, get it in writing, signed by both parties.
- Don't be intimidated by the "Wizard of Oz" methods of collection agencies. There is a computer program—in fact, several—that spits out twenty-six different letters of increasing degrees of severity. The collector is only a computer. If you don't pay after the last letter is sent, the program starts

from scratch. If you do want to pay, there is frequently no one there to deal with. Often these are no more than rip-offs of the creditors who pay for such services. Often, too, real collection agencies handle so many cases with so little attention that you are forgotten from one moment to another. It can take years to make a settlement.

- Many of these turnkey collection businesses are sold to people in worse shape than you who want to start a business on a shoestring and are lucky enough to get a few clients. In such cases, your best bet is to try to negotiate with the creditor directly. Since these collectors have no negotiation skills, it's hard to make a deal.

- When you run into a struggle with a collection agency and settlement is impossible, go directly to your creditor. Agencies get about 20 percent of what they collect. Your creditor can save that amount and pass some of it on to you, if you deal directly. These are hard times and collection is tough and expensive. Some creditors never get paid. A sincere and cooperative debtor is a novelty. Use a counselor or your own ingenuity, but don't leave that debt hanging over your head.

DEBT FOR INVESTMENT

Incurring debt for investment is of an entirely different order than incurring consumer debt. With consumer debt you are using very expensive money. It adds to the price of whatever you buy. The material things get used up, but the debt lingers on. By contrast, incurring debt to make an investment is an important part of building a future and making up for lost time.

A MUFLT LOOK AT HOME MORTGAGES

The role of real estate in making up for lost time is fully discussed in the next chapter. Odds are, however, that your home mortgage is your largest debt. The way we regard mortgages has changed enormously from our parents' generation, and it is changing again.

A mortgage was a burdensome debt to our parents. They aspired to burn it at a celebration sometime in their fifties. The greatest American play of our parents' time was *Death of a Salesman*. At the conclusion of it, Willy Loman's widow stands at his grave and wonders how he could have killed himself when they had just paid off the mortgage.

In our generation, mortgages became a badge of success. The bigger they were, the better. When a house became more valuable, we sold it for a bigger one with a bigger mortgage. Nowadays, the same house is worth less, and the mortgage could be with us forever. There are many benefits to paying off your mortgage early, and there are many convenient ways to do so.

An important part of making up for lost time is the sensible prepayment of your mortgage. You can do it yourself, or you can hire an accountant, buy a $200 computer program, subscribe to a $1,000 service, or ask your mother to do the math. It doesn't matter. Like NIKE, Just Do It. At the very least, get an amortization table from your bank showing how much of your monthly payment is applied to interest as opposed to paying off principal. Even a single extra payment yearly saves thousands in interest.

Getting a Home Mortgage When Your Credit Is Very Poor

In the next chapter I hope to generate some excitement about the future of real estate. If you share my enthusiasm, you will want to be sure that you can get a mortgage. If this is your concern, here are some tips:

1. Direct lenders are more flexible than banks in giving loans to the less creditworthy. Interest rates are often competitive, sometimes a bit higher. Nevertheless, you won't be strapped by narrow lending rules.
2. Go to a bank that knows you. You may be turned down by a stranger bank, but one that handles your business account may extend credit to you.

3. Try FHA. At present, mortgages are available as high as
   $151,725. For details about the ever-changing rules, call the
   FHA at 703-235-8117.

4. Veterans Administration mortgages can be very favorable.

5. Use the numerous resources, books, and seminars to learn
   how to buy foreclosed properties (see the Bibliography).

Debt for Education, Business, and Life Change

Making up for lost time can mean retooling, reeducating, or
waiting out a job loss. There is no better use for credit than investing
in yourself and your family. The only rule is common sense.

FIND FREE MONEY FIRST

Use grant libraries like the Foundation for the Arts, 76 Fifth
Avenue, New York, NY 10011, and any government help you can
find. See Matthew Lesco's *Info-Power* and *Getting Yours* (write: Information USA, Inc. P.O. Box E, Kensington, MD 20895, or call
1-800-955-2702). Borrow only what you must.

KNOW EXACTLY HOW MUCH YOU ARE
BORROWING, AND FOR WHAT

Even if large lines of credit are open to you, don't use them.
You must finance your success, not your failure. There comes a
time when an enterprise is not viable. Don't keep borrowing to
keep an impossible dream alive.

THE LOWEST RATES ARE NOT ALWAYS THE BEST RATES

If you are buying a house, a car, or a coat, by all means take the lowest interest rate you can get. Remember, credit is only a method of "buying" money. Why pay more than you must?

However, if you are buying a business, an education, or weathering a storm, the lender may ask for different types of collateral. A lender who gives you a low-interest business loan and asks for your house as collateral is offering a less desirable deal than one who charges a higher rate and takes only the business as collateral. *In borrowing to invest in yourself, limit your personal liability, even at the expense of interest rates.*

IF CONSUMER SPENDING, CREDIT CARDS, INVESTMENT, OR SPECIAL LOANS RUINED YOUR CREDIT, START TO MAKE UP FOR LOST TIME BY REPAIRING IT NOW

Even if you decide to become a credit "teetotaler," it's important to have a good credit rating. When I went "underground" to investigate the insurance industry, I decided to get a license. I learned that before issuing one, Equifax did a credit check. If you plan to get a job, sign a lease, or seek a Stafford Grant for your college-bound kid, you need a good credit rating. Some people won't even marry you if your credit is bad.

Three large national credit bureaus—Equifax, TRW, and Trans Union Credit Information Company—as well as numerous smaller companies gather credit data. They make it available for a fee to anyone who inquires. In the sixties, when these bureaus first reared their ugly heads, I saw the actor Darren McGavin in a television drama about a man ruined and suicidal because of an erroneous credit report.

I am no friend to credit bureaus. And I've rarely met an institution I didn't like (remember my stint as host of *IRS Tax Beat*?). My animosity stems not from a personal incident, but from the bureaus' method of gathering information. Creditors who subscribe to the service also provide them with information. But every creditor has his own standard of your creditworthiness. Many a person with a poor record looks clean because he or she lucked into lenders who don't report carefully. Another poor Joe, with a good record and a few bad months, can carry a lifetime stigma. The system is unfair, and it is run largely by computer rather than by human head and heart.

Further, anyone with a legitimate "business purpose" can buy a report, i.e., a salesman, marketer, or charity. Such people can also buy "investigative reports," where the bureau can ask your neighbors and others about you. *Consumer Reports* magazine did an investigation of its own. It found that 50 percent of the credit information disseminated on the bureaus' reports was inaccurate. In the past year there have been lawsuits, Attorney General's investigations, and proposed legislation to stop the problem. I hope the effort works. Meanwhile, here is what you must do to help yourself.

GET A COPY OF YOUR CREDIT REPORT FROM EACH BUREAU

Look in the yellow pages and order a copy of your credit from every company listed under the entry for "credit reporting agency or service." In addition, call your local bank and ask which bureaus it uses to check out people seeking mortgages. If you have recently been turned down for credit, the report comes free. If not, the charge is less than $20.

Use John Ventura's book *Fresh Start* as a guide to reading the report and repairing credit. Here are some tips:

1. If you find an error, put it in writing and send copies to the creditor, the collection agency (if any), and the bureau. Enclose any proof you may have of error. Keep copies of all records and correspondence.
2. Under the Fair Credit Property Act (FCPA), the bureau must correct the record after investigation within a reasonable

time. Request that the corrected record be sent to anyone who made an inquiry in the past six months.

3. If no correction is made, the FCPA permits a hundred-word statement from you to be included in the record.

If any information would negatively affect your credit rating

1. It must be deleted if it is seven or more years old (ten, if you went into bankruptcy).
2. The report still can include your own hundred-word explanation.
3. The information can be deleted in exchange for a settlement with the creditor.

If Future Credit Is Part of Your Making-Up-for-Lost-Time Strategy, You Must Rebuild Your Credit

Once you have set the record straight with the reporting companies, you have done enough if you intend to be a credit "teetotaler." However, home ownership and business building are a big part of the MUFLT strategy. Even though I hope you will eschew the credit card, it won't hurt to be creditworthy again. This is most important in getting a low-interest-rate loan. A poor credit risk can still get a loan, but never on favorable terms.

My favorite way to rebuild credit is to open a $500 bank account and then take a passbook loan out against it. In this way you are saving and establishing a good record at the same time. A more dangerous game is to get a bank credit card. These are secured by a deposit and are given to those with poor credit histories. For sources write to BHA, 560 Herndon Parkway, Herndon, VA 22070, or call 1-800-638-6407.

Don't confuse these with the proliferation of merchandise cards, which give you rebates if you buy in their store. I was asked to be a spokesperson for a unique merchandise card. I may do it yet. But it must be able to distinguish itself from a true credit card.

BANKRUPTCY

We have reduced the stigma surrounding alcoholism, drug addiction, and adultery. It seems about time to take the shame out of bankruptcy. Without engaging in a long morality discourse, let me merely quote the Bible:

> At the end of every seven years thou shalt make a release.
> And this is the manner of the release: Every creditor that lendeth ought unto his neighbor shall release it; he shall not exact it of his neighbor or of his brother, because it is called the Lord's release (Deut. 15:1–2)

Despite my feelings about reducing the shame of bankruptcy, I believe that you should avoid it if at all possible. It is still a reputation ruiner. It is hard on the family and kids. It probably is out of keeping with your self-image. I have met numerous businesspeople in bankruptcy. Most of them had a hard time emotionally. Some knew how to play the system like a fiddle. They formed and reformed corporations with no assets and constantly beat their creditors. It is this last small group that gives declaring bankruptcy a slimy aura, when in reality it is a life-saving legal device.

If you are in heavy debt and feel unable to begin again without bankruptcy, please remember that having been a bankrupt will follow you in job applications, loans, and leases. On the other hand, the reporting of a bankruptcy on your credit record must be eliminated after ten years. Once you do go bankrupt, as the Bible says, you cannot do so again for seven years.

Before you talk to a lawyer, read John Ventura, *The Bankruptcy Kit: Understanding the Process, Knowing Your Options, Making a Fresh Start* (Chicago: Dearborn, 1991). Then if you are convinced that bankruptcy is for you, shop for a lawyer who is constantly working in the bankruptcy courts. Even if you have a simple case, hire an expert.

To help demystify the process, these are the answers to the questions on bankruptcy that I am most often asked on my radio shows.

Q: How can I afford a lawyer?

A: *Bankruptcy attorneys will do the work and secure their fee so that they are paid after the bankruptcy along with other creditors. If you have absolutely no assets, see a lawyer who does numerous filings. Lawyers' fees are often under $300 for a "no asset" case. In some areas, your Legal Aid office will handle the case for free. The CCC (see page 204) offices can provide referrals.*

Q: Will I lose my house?

A: *There are several types of bankruptcy. All are governed procedurally by federal statute, but the protection of property is determined by state law. The books I listed earlier and your attorney can tell you which property is exempt from forfeiture in your state of residence. Florida and Texas are very favorable to homeowners; New York and New Jersey are not. Some people establish a new residence before they go bankrupt. If this is done purely to evade creditors, the protection of the laws of the new state that may exempt your house or other assets from loss will not apply. The laws of the state in which you previously lived will dictate the fate of the assets. If, however, you move for the sake of a better job, to downscale, or for some other legitimate purpose, the law of your new state of residence will apply.*

Q: Tell me about the different kinds of bankruptcy. Which ones am I most likely to enter?

A: *A chapter 7 bankruptcy requires you to liquidate all your assets, pay your creditors a portion of the debt, and get fully discharged. This works well if the assets are meager. A chapter 13 should not be called a bankruptcy. Rich people like Donald Trump call it a "workout."*

   Under the law a workout is "an adjustment of debt," in which a plan to pay is worked out. No assets are liquidated unless it is part of the plan. Payment is made over a period of years. The amount to be paid usually is limited to the total value of the assets held by the debtor at the time of filing. The court administers the payments, which may be made over a period of five years. Chapter 13 may not be available to you if your debt-to-asset ratio and your income do not meet certain criteria. However, it is used often and should be explored before going into chapter 7.

Q: What if my creditor is the IRS?

A: *Tax debts are not discharged in bankruptcy. However, you do get a five-year-payout program and forestall all liens, foreclosures, and garnishments.*

Q: Can I rebuild after bankruptcy?

A: *Bankruptcy is a rebuilding in itself. Read articles and books about it and you will find famous athletes, stars, politicians, and (oh yes) several financial experts who went through bankruptcy. And they are all still going strong. Were they lucky or hard-nosed? No. Most cared deeply about being bankrupt, but they were determined to make up for lost time after it was over.*

In reading through my notes and interviews with people I know who went through bankruptcy and emerged a few years later as successes, I was struck by the utter similarity and simplicity of their advice:

Take the opportunity to make totally new priorities. See bankruptcy as a liberating process to seek your dream. Use the freedom to shift your course away from the one that led to the bankruptcy.

Talk about it, but only to those you love and who love you. Never keep your feelings inside, but don't confess all to friends or employers or associates unless they need to know for their own business protection. If you have no loved ones to talk to, try a counselor or a clergy.

Tell your children the truth. Make yourself a shining example of a person who can be a winner even through adversity. One thing that is certain in life is change. Let your children learn as they watch you experiment with legal and emotional ways of changing.

Exercise. All of my bankruptcy successes took new care of their bodies during and after bankruptcy. It was something they could control, and they needed the physical strength to manage the stress. In my research I've met many successful former bankrupts. When I meet someone who's been through bankruptcy and has reestablished himself, I know I'm in the presence of a strong and admirable survivor.

C H A P T E R   2 1

INSURANCE DURING THE

"MAKING-UP" YEARS

My idea of purgatory is being locked up in a room with an insurance agent.

WOODY ALLEN

GOING UNDERGROUND IN THE INSURANCE INDUSTRY

For eighteen months I was a spy in the insurance industry. I worked for Met Life, one of the largest and most prestigious insurance companies in the world. To be fair, I did not consider myself a spy, nor did I intend it. It was the late eighties. My radio station, WMCA, had been sold to a religious organization and I needed a new job. If I opened my law practice again, I knew that I would not be free to go back into media if the call came. An ad in *The New York Law Journal* offered jobs to lawyers who also knew personal finance. I took the position, studied for the test, and learned more about insurance as a product, an industry, a business, and an American institution than I could have learned from any book.

As a real-life, although inadvertent, investigative reporter, I have formed many opinions about the industry, most of which you are about to read. Let me make this disclaimer: *The opinions expressed below are not necessarily those of the insurance industry or those of the anti-insurance industry. They are solely the opinions of the author.*

OPINION 1:THE INSURANCE INDUSTRY COULD BE THE SINGLE GREATEST PERSONAL FINANCE ADVISORY IN THE WORLD IF ITS PROFITS WERE MADE FROM SERVICE, NOT SALES.

If you don't buy from an insurance agent, he or she will not be paid for the considerable effort put into advising you. By its very nature, insurance advice is a selling tool. What's more, commissions are based on the type of product you buy and how much of it you buy. Even more than stockbrokers, insurance agents are biased by their own monetary interests.

This is a shame. For the most part, insurance salespeople of all ranks are intelligent, well-informed, and passionate about helping you. They are not a predatory group, and in general they believe in doing well by doing good. They have information on everything from taxes to mortality at their fingertips. Nevertheless, unless they "bill" themselves as financial planners, they can't make a living just by helping you. They also know that you are resistant to making a purchase that admits, and plans for, your mortality. That's why many of them disguise themselves as planners, thereby giving both disciplines a bad name.

OPINION 2: THE ANTI-INSURANCE INDUSTRY, IN THE GUISE OF CONSUMER ADVOCACY, HAS LEFT MANY AN ORPHAN AND WIDOW ON THE POVERTY LINE.

Make no mistake, so-called consumer advocates who trash everything but the most minimal insurance coverage are no friend to you. One can always make money in personal finance by trashing the IRS and the insurance industry. Everyone thinks such gurus are sincere; after all, what can they possibly have to gain? How about book royalties, columns, publicity, and in one case a fat job in the industry just to shut up? Don't allow so-called consumer advocates and scare tactics to cause you to underbuy.

OPINION 3: IF YOU ARE IN THE MAKING-UP-FOR-LOST-TIME YEARS, YOU ARE LIKELY TO BE BOTH UNDERINSURED AND PAYING TOO MUCH—THE WORST OF BOTH WORLDS.

If you have dependents and you are over forty, a top priority must be to insure your life so they can flourish if you meet an early death. There, I used the D word. Term insurance through your employment is not enough. The death benefit is usually too low, and the cost of converting the policy is often high if you leave the job. In some cases, if you, instead of your employer, pay for your group coverage, you might be able to get a better deal independently.

To insure your family's future in the event of your demise, buy convertible, renewable term insurance. This is death-benefit-only insurance; it builds up no cash surrender value. Its purpose is purely to pay off in the event that you die. Make sure it is renewable all your life unless you know that your dependents will not need your income if you die after a certain age. Make sure that you can convert it into whole life (see *Opinion 6*) if it fits your needs. Hence its name: renewable, convertible term insurance.

Buy term with premiums that are guaranteed for at least five years. If you are over fifty and have young children, make it fifteen years. It's more expensive to begin with, but you will not get any renewal-cost surprises at a time when the death benefit is still critical to your family's survival.

Such insurance is very economical. A fortyish person in fair health can leave $1 million for well under $1,000 a year. Which brings me to my next, and most controversial, opinion.

OPINION 4: EVERY FORTYSOMETHING FAMILY NEEDS AT LEAST $500,000 IN DEATH BENEFITS.

There are all kinds of methods for determining the precise amount of coverage to buy for each employed provider in the family. The National Insurance Consumer Organization (NICO) recommends that it be a multiple of seven times your income. Jane Bryant Quinn credits financial planner John Allen of Arvada, Colorado, with a nicely worked-out (but labor-intensive) method of determining how much is enough for you. See her book *Making the Most of Your Money* (New York: Simon & Schuster, 1991) for fifteen pages of small print on how to determine your family's needs when you are gone.

Or you can do it my way. First, go into a quiet room. Think about your family's lifestyle. How much do you think they will need to continue that lifestyle? Did you save any money to leave as an inheritance? If you die, are they left high and dry financially? Calculate what other income will come in without you there. Is there a big mortgage to pay? College coming up? Other debts? What figure feels right? Put needs, debts, and income potential together. What total inheritance would you like to leave? What figure makes you comfortable? That's your peace-of-mind-target death benefit.

Next, comparison-shop to get the best price on the death benefit you choose. Also, compare pricing procedure, which is not unlike car pricing. Contact NICO for the latest cost statistics. Consult a financial planner who works with at least four insurance companies and ask for price quotes, or see a general agent who can deal with many companies. Ask your bank about Savings Bank Life Insurance. Get costs on the same amount of renewable, convertible term insurance from similarly rated companies, or from insurance quote firms such as Select Quote. Buy the cheapest!

OPINION 5: CANCEL YOUR INSURANCE AS SOON AS YOUR
EARNINGS ARE NOT NEEDED TO KEEP THE FAMILY GOING,
BUT USE JOINT-AND-SURVIVOR INSURANCE TO LEAVE A
LEGACY.

Term insurance is bought to keep your family going in the event that you die during the making-up-for-lost-time process. If you become a huge financial success or if the family grows up and becomes independent, the insurance has fulfilled its purpose and can be canceled.

If you want, as I would, to leave an insurance death benefit anyway, in the nature of a large legacy for your children, grandchildren, or other beloveds, you cannot rely on the term policy. Many are extinguished when you reach age seventy, and if you are lucky enough to partake of the new longevity, you will outlive the legacy-bestowing policy. Even those that stay in force become too expensive by the time you reach your late fifties. The cost of the legacy will retard the growth of your Three-Tier investment program.

Instead, try a "second-to-die" or "joint-and-survivor" policy. These policies are part term and part whole life (see *Opinion 6*). They pay off only when the survivor of the joint policy dies. Since there are two measuring lives, the underwriting is more liberal. In the event that one person has a medical problem, a joint policy is easier to get than an individual policy. Further, if one person is younger than the other, even by only a year or two, the cost of the policy is quite low compared to an individual policy.

Since both parties, usually spouses, must die before the policy pays, joint-and-survivor is really a legacy tool for the children and grandchildren, or a method of paying taxes if you manage to make up for lost time in a big way. Before you buy the policy, you should first create an insurance trust to own the policy. Many people believe that death-benefit insurance is not estate-taxable when the insured dies. Not true. It is 100 percent includable in the decedent's gross estate. With certain deductions, it is part of the figure that is used to calculate the tax. If a trust owns the policy and distributes the proceeds to your heirs, however, they will receive the bounty tax-free. If the money is needed to pay taxes on other assets, the trust document allows your heirs to lend funds to the estate to pay death taxes.

After you have begun to make up for lost time, I hope you will graduate to estate planning. See the Bibliography for some good books on this subject.

In short, my favorite insurance play for making up for lost time is a hefty term policy and a reasonably priced second-to-die policy: the former to protect against the financial risk of early death; the latter to leave a legacy that you probably will not be able to duplicate by saving and investing.

If you are an individual without a spousal partner or business partner and still want to leave a death benefit as a legacy, you cannot buy second-to-die, as it requires joint lives. Instead, you must use some form of whole life policy. This is the area of insurance planning where you will feel the most anxiety. I don't blame you. Here is my opinion.

Opinion 6: Never Buy Any Financial Product You Do Not Fully Understand; Therefore, You Probably Cannot Buy Whole Life Insurance.

This opinion is deliberately calculated to encourage the insurance industry to disclose and explain all aspects of whole life insurance to the consuming public and not use obfuscating jargon and cryptic illustrations.

Whole life insurance is completely different from term. Your premiums stay level (see the variations in *Opinion 7*), and a portion is invested for you by the insurance company. That portion grows, tax-deferred. You have already read about using whole life to build a private pension. It can work. But as you shop for policies, you will learn that finding accurate information about the costs and benefits of this insurance is a difficult pursuit.

Your agent will give you insurance illustrations that show you the premiums, the death benefit, the projected cash value, the date at which you no longer must pay premiums (vanish date), and more. Some of the problems with this are

- The illustrations may presume your good health and show a lower premium than you eventually are offered.
- The agent can select a dividend rate that may not be reasonable.
- It is almost impossible to understand what fraction of your premium is being used for investment as opposed to death benefit.
- It is almost impossible to know the actual total return so that you can compare it with the return on other investments.
- While you can borrow from a policy, often the amount you borrow does not earn dividends even though you are paying interest on the loan.

Note: this borrowing power is crucial to the use of insurance as a pension alternative. Always buy a policy that continues to accumulate dividends on borrowed funds.

As a result of the policy's complexity, aided by the sales techniques of some agents, many experts steer you away from whole life. Most of my writing and media colleagues preach "term only." It's too bad because the right whole life policy can help make up for lost time.

OPINION 7: IF YOU ARE IN A HIGH TAX BRACKET, HAVE FUNDED OTHER TAX-DEFERRED PROGRAMS, AND HAVE ADDITIONAL INVESTMENT DOLLARS, TRY WHOLE LIFE.

Whole life in all its many incarnations is for those who are comfortable diversifying their investments through the use of insurance. There are several types of whole life, each with an investment component.

A particularly flexible form of whole life is *universal life*. You start with a target premium, but each year you can contribute more or less within a given range. You can apply the premium to death benefit or cash accumulation. In that way you control which grows faster. But beware: Universal life is a load product, meaning that a portion of the premium goes to pay costs and commissions.

Your cash accumulation earns an interest rate that is tied to an index and may be guaranteed for a year or more. This is a Tier-One investment. A related policy called *variable universal life* allows you to invest in a series of growth funds instead. This fits into Tier-Two investing. In either case, some companies deduct additional commissions, costs, and fees from these earnings.

To get a semiaccurate idea of what you are really getting, ask your planner or NICO for the "internal interpolated yield." This provides the policy's yield while taking into account its costs. The current cost of the service is $35 for one policy and $25 thereafter. I suggest that you pay the price and check it out before you buy.

When retirement rolls around, you can withdraw up to the amount of the premium that you paid for tax-free, as a return of principal. You can then borrow out the remaining cash value at a compounding interest rate. At present, this interest rate is not deductible from your income tax.

Another variation on this theme is *variable life*, in which the premiums are guaranteed. There is also a guaranteed minimum death benefit regardless of how well the investments do. Unlike whole life, however, variable life does not return a guaranteed interest rate. Instead, your money is invested in a separate account and grows according to the management expertise applied to the funds in that account. Unlike universal life, you determine the underlying investment vehicle, including growth funds, aggressive growth funds, bonds, and even zero-coupon bonds.

Variable life also permits you to opt for a guaranteed interest rate if you are willing to allow your funds to become part of the assets of the company. Again, this is our familiar Tier-One investment. You are lending your money to the insurance company in return for a guaranteed interest rate.

There are hybrids of this variation. A straight variable life policy affords a fixed yearly premium. A universal variable life policy allows the flexibility of premium offered in the universal life policy. Some companies call these scheduled and flexible variable life, respectively.

Of the investment-oriented policies, it is universal life that has gotten a black eye in the past. The premiums devoted to investments are part of the general assets of the company, not segregated in a separate account for you. Therefore, the assets are subject to the claims of the companies' creditors. Investment results were in the control of and could be manipulated by the company's reporting methods.

Your accumulated amount goes up and down with the market; so does the death benefit. If performance is poor, you may have to put in extra premiums to maintain the level of insurance you need. There are often caps that apply. For example, in some cases you must earn at least 4 percent or more in order for the death benefit to increase.

If the past performance of a company is excellent in its investment results, if you have a need for life insurance, and if you are on the young side of the making-up-for-lost-time crowd, variable insurance may work for you. This is especially true if you are the type to be better disciplined in paying for insurance than in contributing to a mutual fund and buying term. Investing through insurance can also work well as an addition (and occasionally an alternative) to pension plans.

Opinion 8: For Some of Us Who Are Making Up for Lost Time, Whole Life Insurance Is a Brilliant Choice.

The varieties of whole life insurance, particularly in variable life insurance that allow you to invest in the stock market, can be a brilliant Tier-Two investment! For whom?

If you are a business owner with employees, you may, by law, have to cover many of them under a pension plan if you create one for yourself. This prevents many entrepreneurs from starting a tax-deferred program. You already know that you probably cannot make up for lost time without one. Yet you can doom a fragile new business to failure if employees are required to be included in the plan.

An alternative is to buy a variable life policy and make your contributions to the premiums. These are insurance policies, not pensions, so they are not subject to pension rules. Yet, like pensions, they accumulate tax-deferred. Moreover, you may take the money out tax-free as a return of capital (up to the amount of your premiums) at any age. If you are incorporated, you can even deduct the cost of the premiums from earnings of the company. Naturally, you must include the premiums as income on your personal tax return.

Opinion 9: Ordinary Whole Life Policies (Straight Life and Permanent Life) Are of Limited Appeal.

These are the standard policies that accumulate cash value and death benefit at a given yearly premium. The investment portion of the premium is invested by the company in Tier-One-type products. Eventually you can use the dividends to help pay the premium. Sales charges can be more than 50 percent of the first year's premium. People are attracted to this type of policy because the premium stays steady and eventually will vanish (dividends pay the cost). But it is very costly insurance. As for the use of cash value for your retirement, it's like investing in Tier Ones at a higher commission. The tax breaks are usually not worth it.

OPINION 10: YOU MUST HAVE DISABILITY INSURANCE.

If you are in the age range to make up for lost time, your risk of becoming disabled is at least five times your risk of dying. Disability insurance in our age bracket is not a luxury; it is a necessity. The selection of the policy has largely to do with who you are as a person.

Policies differ depending on your occupation. The costs and the coverage are dictated by your "class of employment." This status is not in your control once you have chosen your career.

A decision that you can control, however, is the definition of "disability." This determines what must happen to you in order for you to collect. Some policies (the cheapest) pay if you can't perform any work. Some policies (the most expensive) pay if your ability to perform even a single aspect of your present employment is impaired. If you were disabled, what would you do? Retool, take a similar but less hectic career? Be a free-lancer? Teach in your existing field? The more your life options, the less coverage you need and the cheaper the policy will be.

A second decision you must make relates to the time at which you need the disability income to start. If you have no savings to weather a storm, the policy may be needed immediately. If you can wait three months or more, you can buy a considerably less-expensive policy that doesn't pay off immediately upon disability.

Another consideration is the availability of disability at work and through Social Security. Your human resources director can advise you on this.

A final consideration is the amount that your family needs to live on if you become disabled. Remember, disability benefits will come to you tax-free. So when you make your analysis, you need not provide for taxes on the policy benefits.

MAKING UP FOR LOST TIME MEANS
UNDERSTANDING YOUR COVERAGE

All the opinions I have expressed stem from our need to balance cost against adequate coverage. As we make up for lost time, we want the freedom to pour funds into wealth-building tools. At the same time, we must manage the risks of ill health, disability, and death. For you to do this adequately without spending all your time on insurance management, you must take three steps: (1) know your present coverage, (2) know the safety of the companies with which you are doing business, and (3) shop with consumer wisdom.

In the Introduction I complained that the language of money is not always poetry. Nothing is more cut-and-dried than marshaling the facts regarding insurance. And in this chapter, I've given you some facts and pointers about different kinds of policy coverage. But what about insurance companies?

WILL YOUR INSURANCE COMPANY BE THERE
WHEN YOU NEED IT?

Only recently has the idea of institutional risk sat so heavily upon us. To begin to evaluate an insurance institution's safety, you must consider the safety-rating system that is used in the insurance industry. Companies that are rated must pay an independent service to include them in the ratings. At present, the largest rating service is A. M. Best. To pass the first test of safety, a company should at least receive the highest Best rating (triple-A).

Following Best is Standard & Poor's. It ranks seventy-five companies, concentrating on the company's ability to pay claims. Its rating system goes from a high of triple-A to a low of D. More than 50 percent of the companies are rated triple-A. Duff and Phelps ranks twenty-eight to thirty-five companies, giving top ratings to only six. Moody's ranks forty-six to fifty companies, its ratings being triple-A to C. Townsend and Schupp ranks seventy-five companies in ten categories such as dividend performance, pretax earnings, debts, and investment performance.

All of these ratings can be provided for you by an insurance agent. Or you can order a rating report for $15 from Weiss Research, Inc., 2200 North Florida Mango Road, West Palm Beach, FL 33409; 1-800-289-9222. If the company has not ranked high with most of the rating services for at least five years, it has failed safety test number one.

If it does rank high, go on to safety test number two. Check the following facts about the company:

- Surplus—What are the company's assets over its liabilities?
- Mandatory securities reserve—Is the ratio of the surplus to the mandatory reserve 6 percent or better (it should be)?
- Kinds of assets—Do the company's assets include junk bonds and bad real estate?
- Investment return—What is the company's investment return over a five-year period?
- Dividends—Where are the company's dividends coming from, earnings or surplus,?
- Low-interest loans—Does the company have low-interest loans out against the policies? Such loans bring little revenue to the company and may be made to support low-performing subsidiary companies.
- Persistency—Are customers canceling policies?

All of this information is available from A. M. Best and can be found in the reference section of your library and from your insurance agent as well.

If the facts look good, go on to safety test number three. Call NICO and ask for its review. If you are satisfied on all three scores, buy the policy.

This information is designed to help you select a company and a policy, not to intimidate you or give you cold feet. The worst thing you can do to your family is leave them uninsured. I know a little girl whose father died suddenly at age forty-two and left the family with no protection. Even though he was a high-salaried attorney, he never took the time to focus on his insurance needs. That was my father. Don't let it be your child's father or mother. Dreary as it seems, bite the bullet and use your new knowledge— don't avoid or unduly delay buying a policy, or reviewing the policy you already have.

REAL ESTATE AND REALITY

101: YOUR OWN HOME

A man's home is his castle. (But it can also be his prison.)

ADRIANE G. BERG

Home ownership is the centerpiece of the American Dream, as well it should be. No matter what happened in the early nineties to the value of our home, most of us agree that our home is still our best investment. With the development of cooperatives and condominiums, which are as carefree and compact as apartment living, singles as well as couples are finding their way to home ownership. Not only do I believe that home ownership is part of making up for lost time, but I believe that it is a premier goal in itself, even if you don't resell at a profit.

Less than five years ago, every family had home ownership as a major priority. Today, I fear, this dream is slipping away. You will hear many experts touting the virtues of renting instead of owning. Don't listen to them.

Naturally, many people lost their taste for real estate because the wild increase in prices of the eighties gave them a false sense of security about the value of their homes. The brightest of us took mortgages on first and second homes way over their eventual market value. By 1992, foreclosures were rampant. In 1993, a friend of mine who is a receiver in bankruptcy told me that the banks in her area were not foreclosing. Property values were so low that they had no way to sell the property.

Nevertheless, while it is true that expectations of increased wealth solely through home ownership have greatly diminished, I still believe strongly in home ownership. If you do not yet own a home, or if you do and are thinking of becoming a renter instead, these are my arguments for becoming or staying a home owner.

Damage Control.

A renter is at the mercy of the landlord and the rental market. If rents go up, a carefully planned budget is cast to the winds. Rent is a wild card in the making-up-for-lost-time game. So are adjustable-rate mortgages and cooperative-maintenance charges. But while you can pass up adjustable rates and stay away from co-ops with a history of maintenance hikes, you can't control your rent.

Inflation.

One thing is clear: When inflation rises, so do housing values. In the event of inflation, home ownership gives you many options; renting gives you only a headache. The options include (1) selling your home and downscaling to a fully paid-up residence, (2) borrowing wisely to finance college or other dreams, and (3) shopping in less inflated areas for more real estate and using an equity loan or new mortgage to afford a downpayment. This is the essence of the old "no money down" idea, which still works if it's used wisely.

At Present, Home Owners Can Leave Their Children a Substantial Inheritance.

Under today's Internal Revenue Code, real estate is one of the assets where an heir receives a "stepped-up basis." This means that property that has appreciated is deemed to be received by an heir at the market price of the property at the date of death of the decedent, not at the price that the decedent paid when he or she bought the property. If Dad paid $50,000 for a home now worth $100,000 and left it to Junior, Junior is deemed to have paid

$100,000. If he sells at the date-of-death value, he pays no capital gains tax on the profit. In fact, an executor can elect to deem the value at the date six months after the death. That can be wise if the value grows in that period of time after death, making the evaluation more favorable to the heir.

Home Ownership Comes with Other Tax Benefits.

Although I believe in early mortgage prepayment, while you are paying, the interest is tax-deductible. Local real estate land taxes may be onerous, but at least they are federally tax-deductible too.

Home Ownership Is a Leverage Power Tool.

In my discussion of speed investing and again in the chapters on debt and credit, the concept of leverage is explored. Leverage is the power to buy a more valuable asset with a small amount of cash. All real estate is a leverage power tool. You'll find a full discussion of leverage as it applies to real estate in the next chapter.

The Great Gatsby Is Gone Forever.

Most of us are sour on real estate as a backlash to our profligate ways of the eighties. Real estate ownership is so tangible and so ego-boosting that many of us happily put all of our financial eggs in the real estate basket. Many of us also relied entirely on the resale value of our homes for our retirement future. We went overboard in debt, in cost, and in expectation. If we learned anything from the recession of the early nineties, it was never to do that again. But let's not throw out the baby with the bathwater. Home ownership as part, but not all, of our making-up-for-lost-time program is a smart move.

Psychological Benefit.

Real estate is shelter. Food, clothing, and shelter are life's three fundamentals for survival. Most people have a nesting instinct and feel proud to own their own homes. They are uncomfortable as renters. (Many New Age prosperity thinkers do not believe in individual home ownership. They strive for community. I believe this to be a flaw in an otherwise valuable movement.)

How to Buy Your Own Home Cheap and Fast

The best time to buy any real estate is in a bad market. In 1991, after trying to sell my New York cooperative apartment for three years without success, I got an acceptable offer with one catch: I had to move out within a month. I was seven months pregnant and working over forty hours a week. A month earlier, my husband had taken a new job in New Jersey and was reverse-commuting every day. I took the offer as an omen that it was time to move. I made the one-month deadline, and bought a beautiful home in the town where my husband had his office, for $40,000 under the market price. Here's how to do it.

Take a map and a protractor. Pinpoint the place to which you must commute each day. Draw a circle with its radius the number of miles you are willing to travel to get to work. (If you are a working couple this might involve reaching a compromise.) Next, if you commute by bus or train, get a timetable and circle the communities that are inside the circle you have drawn and have a good commuter timetable that fits your needs.

Now, if you have children, call the board of education in the communities that fit your commuting requirements. Find out about the schools—the ratio of children to teachers, the number of books in the library, whether special programs exist for kids with special needs, and where the kids go to college after graduating from the local high school. Pick as many communities that meet your standards as you can.

With a list of your target communities in hand, work with two brokers in each area. Tell them that you are interested in buying properties that

Are owned and being sold by a relocation service because the owners have already moved

Are being sold by an estate

Are being sold as a result of a divorce or other special circumstances

Are being sold as is because of their need to be fixed up

Are distressed in some other way

Work only with brokers who agree to show you the "properties sold" book. This is not the multiple-listing book that shows houses for sale. This is the book that shows houses that have already sold. The amount of time it took to make the sale, the original asking price, and the eventual sale price are all listed. This is the best way for you to find out if you are really getting a good deal compared to other properties.

Brokers are not enough. In addition, you must look in three other ways: real estate owned (REO), for sale by owner (FISBO), and foreclosures. An REO is real estate owned by a bank that had to foreclose on it. When this happens frequently, a bank loses its reputation. With a severe REO problem, the bank will go into receivership and be taken over by the Resolution Trust Corporation (RTC).

For this reason, banks do not shout REOs from the roof-tops. You must inquire. The bank may even deny having any. Just politely explain that you intend to move into the neighborhood if you can do business with them. You are a ready buyer who has done the research. Further, you plan to bank there when you move in. Even ask to speak with the president of the bank. Explain that this is not a fishing expedition; you are serious. In most cases, it may take five to ten phone calls. Don't give up.

Negotiate for both price and terms. Although I didn't buy it, I could have bought a mansion on the same block to which I moved with an 8 percent mortgage from a local bank. I passed it up only because I was too pregnant and busy to do the fixing up it needed to meet my standards. But it was a great buy. If the bank sends you to a broker handling its REO property, don't despair. Work with the broker.

A FISBO can also be a good buy. You should at the very least save the brokerage fee. Negotiations often are very touchy, however.

It takes an experienced, unemotional buyer to deal with an inexperienced, emotional seller. Try anyway. Find FISBOs by looking for signs in front of a house indicating it is for sale. Always cruise neighborhoods you like to find these signs. You also can find FISBOs from ads in the newspapers and by ringing the doorbell of a home you like and asking if it's for sale.

Don't be horrified by my last suggestion. I've made every mistake in the book and want you to learn from my experience. Real estate is not a subject to be shy about. I missed the mews house of my dreams in Greenwich Village because I didn't tell my friend how much I wanted her house. She never told me that she wanted to sell. One day, I learned that she had sold with no money down for $25,000 below market to a stranger.

Finally, call the courthouse and find out the name of the "legal paper." This is the newspaper that the law requires to carry ads for auctions, sheriff's sales, and foreclosures. Up to the date of sale, you can negotiate directly with the owners. You can inspect the premises, sign a contract, and get financing. You also can wait until the sale and perhaps get the property cheaper. But you will need to bring cash, take the property as is, pass a credit check before you can bid, and get financing fast. Still, it's worth getting the knack of foreclosure buying, especially if you plan to help make up for lost time by investing in real estate. I will discuss foreclosures in more detail in the next chapter.

Two More Super Secrets for Buying Your Own Home Cheap and Fast

Super Secret 1: Make Friends with the Owner of a Title Insurance Company.

In many states, a lender and purchaser do not simply sign a mortgage. Instead, a trust deed is signed, with a real estate title company as trustee. If the mortgage borrower doesn't pay, the trustee intervenes for a speedy foreclosure. In trust deed states, title companies have notice of all properties they handle that are about to be foreclosed upon. Even in nontrust deed states, they have notice of a fair number. It is legal to solicit a list and even to pay a finder's fee if you buy one.

Super Secret 2: Contact a Relocation Service Directly.

If you have chosen an area with an industrial park or other corporate enterprise, chances are that the corporations that employ people in the area relocate them as well. If so, they will have an in-house or outside relocation service. That service wants to relocate executives, not sell real estate. It wants to remove the inventory from its books. I bought a Manhattan co-op directly from a relocation service at $100,000 below-market (honest) just because it wanted to get rid of its book entry before the end of the year.

Financing Your Purchase

If your problem in buying a home is not purchase price, but financing, there are also a number of solutions for you. Most important, pull out all the stops. Borrow from your pension and from your family, and tighten your belt. I have never known anyone focused on buying a home who couldn't do it. Perhaps you will have to compromise on what you buy, but you will buy. Here are some ideas for financing the purchase.

REVENUE SHARING

See Chapter 19 on borrowing from and lending to family members. You may at least get a down payment by offering family members a fractional interest in your home, a second mortgage with interest, and if they are part owner, even giving them the real estate tax deductions.

FHA REPOSSESSIONS

The federal government repossesses properties that it accepted as collateral for loans. A property often sells for no more than 5 to

7 percent below the market value, but, if you plan to live in it, you often get a low-interest-rate mortgage and a 5 percent downpayment. The FHA will give you a list of properties, as will some local brokers. Remember, much of this property was FHA-financed because the areas needed rehabilitation. If the location is no good or if the place is dilapidated, pass it up. Unless you are a martyr, the burden of fixing up the property and coping with the neighborhood may be too much for you. Besides, times have changed. Only the better properties will make money on resale in this post-1990 market.

DIRECT LENDERS AND MORTGAGE BROKERS

If your income is low or your credit is poor, you can still borrow money, but for a price. Read Chapter 20 on credit for sensible ways to handle your borrowing. Borrowing is really buying money. It may be worth borrowing at a high price and prepaying to cut down overall interest charges. In this way, you get your home, reestablish your credit, and cut the ultimate cost of borrowing by paying early and refinancing when your credit is repaired.

NO MONEY DOWN

Notice that what was once a national movement is now only a few paragraphs in this book. If you have no down payment and/or a poor credit record, you may be able to get seller financing from a motivated seller. The less you have to offer, the more desperate the seller must be in order to be willing to do business.

The nineties is the reality decade in real estate. Don't believe the salespeople in the 2:00 A.M. TV infomercials who tell you that it's easy to make a no-money-down fortune. These sellers are difficult to find. Look for properties that have been owned by a seller for many years. In these cases, you may be dealing with people who have paid off their mortgage and don't need a down payment to clear their loan. You may also be dealing with an older person who may want to retire and would like income secured by his or her property rather than cash that can only be reinvested at low interest rates.

An aggressive no-money-down buyer can purchase a list of home owners in a specific area who are of retirement age. These lists cost from $40 to $85 per thousand names. You can do a mass mailing soliciting a response. If one in one thousand answers, you may have your home with no money down. How do you find the sellers of these lists? Look in the yellow pages under "list brokers."

Finally, if all else fails, be a renter in your primary residence and buy a second home in a resort area. You can rent it to others and/or use it for your own enjoyment. If you pick the right area, you can retire there and it will eventually be your primary residence.

Above all, if you must rent, move to a single-family residence and offer a lease purchase. Part of your rent goes to a down payment on the property. You set a purchase price and a purchase date. If you fail to buy, the seller keeps the extra rent. If you do buy, the additional rent is deducted from the purchase price. Meanwhile, the seller cannot sell to anyone else, and the purchase price is frozen regardless of the market at the purchase date. If you make such a deal, tighten your belt, repair your credit, and prepare to buy.

And now let's turn to the next chapter to see how you can make up for lost time by finding your fortune in investment real estate.

REAL ESTATE AND REALITY 102: INVESTING FOR THE FUTURE

When at first you don't succeed, buy, buy again.

ADRIANE G. BERG

An investment in real estate with realistic expectations is one of your best bets for making up for lost time. To make large profits in real estate, you must have a new understanding of the three factors that make real estate a must in making up for lost time: (1) leverage, (2) inflation, and (3) the Three-Tier nature of real estate. Once you know these factors, you can select the tier in which you want your real estate to function and can chart a specific plan for investing in that tier.

THE LATEST WORD ON LEVERAGE

The feature most attractive about real estate is the ability to buy a parcel valued way beyond the cash you have on hand. A lender or the seller gives you a loan, using the real estate itself as the security. In this way real estate is its own collateral. Nothing has changed since the heydays of the eighties except for a healthy skepticism over whether the real estate will appreciate at a greater pace than the debt you take on to buy it.

If you understand how leverage helps make up for lost time, you won't overborrow to buy real estate. Let's say you have $20,000 to invest and you buy a mutual fund. If the fund appreciates by 10 percent, you have made $2,000. Not bad.

If you invested the same $20,000 in a real estate parcel, it's likely that you could buy one worth $100,000 (this is so because a conservative investor will finance only 80 percent of the cost of a real estate purchase.) Let's say that again the investment rose 10 percent. Now, with a $20,000 investment, you have made not $2,000, as with the mutual fund, but $20,000. The gain is yours on the entire $100,000 value.

Throughout the eighties, Americans bought real estate, understandably enamored of this concept. Some ended up millionaires. Others went bankrupt. Yet the concept of leverage was the same for all of them. The great difference between the real estate winners and losers can be found in the way they handled leverage. Here's how the winners did it.

First, Winners Knew How Much of a Profit They Could Expect and Took It. Losers Looked for Unlimited Wealth with a Small Down Payment.

When the market value of real estate went up, winners sold and took a real profit. They paid taxes and reinvested their profits in Tier-One or Tier-Two investments. Today they have a high net worth. They knew that real estate is cyclical and that no boom lasts forever.

Losers were content with paper profits. When their real estate went up, they took a loan out against it at a high interest rate. They disregarded the facts: that the benefits of leverage are diminished by the interest-rate cost of financing, that markets change, and that the real estate could some day be worth less than the financed sum.

Most important, losers did not know about long-term-investment pace. Over time, real estate averages 6 percent a year growth. They did not realize that the eighties were an aberrant period in which to make hay, but one that would surely come to an end. Winners knew this and took profits for safety.

Second, Winners Selected Real Estate Based on Quality. Losers Selected the Parcel with the Greatest Leverage.

Many properties are distressed, usually for a reason like poor condition or location. Under these circumstances, sellers may take back large, even 100 percent mortgages in order to sell. Hence, no money down. Losers bought whatever they could get their hands on with little cash, regardless of the quality of the property. If they flipped (sold the property quickly or sold the contract to purchase before they closed), they may have made a fast profit. This is not so different from any of our Tier-Three speculations. Many did not sell, however; they kept the property and the high debt too long. The market value declined and the debt remained. The result has been a record number of foreclosures and abandonments.

In contrast, the winners bought for value. Many still have their properties in good locations or with high rent rolls. They can get as much or more on the sale of those properties as they paid years ago. They know that leverage alone is not enough.

Third, Winners Expected to Work Hard for Their Profits. Losers Expected to Get Rich Quick.

In the eighties, many losers believed in the "greater fool theory": A fool greater than they would come along and pay even more than they did for the property! And there were many such fools. A few made money. More by accident than by design.

But most who made lasting profits knew what they were doing. They had the market timed right, and they knew how to select and manage property. They were also savvy about kinds of "distress": A seller in trouble was an opportunity. A property in trouble was a liability.

FOURTH, LOSERS DID NOT REALIZE THAT THEY WERE
EXPECTING TIER-THREE RESULTS FROM A TIER-TWO RISK.

Winners knew that buying highly leveraged real estate is akin
to a Tier-Three speculation. They knew that in order to make
money fast with high leverage, they had to turn over the property
and make a profit quick. It can be done. If they missed their chances,
they had to be financially prepared to wait perhaps fifteen years for
the next turnaround. To be a high-leverage winner, you must see
a ready resale market within eighteen months to two years of your
purchase.

A LOOK AT INFLATION AND REAL ESTATE

It has long been conventional wisdom that real estate values go
up as inflation rises. Therefore, it acts as a hedge against inflation.
This is true. But for the average investor, these results show up
only on paper. This is because, like all investments, real estate is
cyclical, and the cycle is long. The investor who does not carefully
track the market will not sell at the peak time.

In our time we saw

1972–75 a slow market

1976–80 a very strong market

1981–85 a declining market

1986–88 a boom

1989–93 a decline

1994– a slowly increasing market

These are national outlooks and therefore may be quite different
in your specific area. When it comes to the real estate market, as
we learned in *The Music Man*, "You've got to know the territory!"
You must be familiar with both the local market and the national
inflation. The average property owner counts his blessings during

an inflation, but never sells and counts his money. This is particularly true if the property in question is his own home. The increased market value in a primary residence is meaningless unless the homeowner is ready to sell.

To make best use of inflationary trends to make up for lost time with real estate, go back to the economic indicators suggested in Chapter 14. The indicators will show when to sell. The value of real estate in virtually all locations rises with inflation. Even if you choose not to sell, you can make money if you own rentable property. Rents rise with inflation, too. Long leases can bring you high income that lasts longer than the inflationary period. If you are five or more years from retirement, don't sell. Keep your property and add to your income stream.

Here, then, are the new rules for making up for lost time with real estate.

1. Use Leverage. Be aware of the cost of the money you borrow. Be sure that the property is quickly salable and that your debt period will be short. If you plan to keep the property, be sure that the rent roll will pay the debt. Never rely on ever-increasing property values or inflation to justify the use of leverage.

2. Withdraw Equity from Real Estate Judiciously. If the value of your property rises, don't automatically borrow to buy more property. You are turning equity into debt unless the parcel you buy is of equal potential to what you own. Use the same good judgment the second time around as you did the first.

3. Know the Business. By all means buy property through distress sales and foreclosures. But don't believe in fairy tales. A distressed property usually has a downside.

4. Buy Quality. Perhaps the most exciting change in real estate investment is the new definition of quality and desirability. There is money to be made recognizing what Americans want today.

5. Diversify. Don't give up cash flow or tie up all your assets for a real estate purchase.

6. Protect Your Children's Inheritance. If you plan to leave real estate to your children, make sure that there is enough liquidity or enough of an insurance policy to pay the estate taxes. Taxes are due within nine months of death. If the dollars are not there, the real estate must be sold immediately to pay the tax.

THE THREE-TIER METHOD OF GETTING RICH OVERNIGHT WITH REAL ESTATE (JUST KIDDING!)

Seriously, folks, there are three ways to make money in real estate. They correspond to our Three-Tier method. The first is to buy at a fair price, and rent for income through the years. Perhaps you may never sell such Tier-One real estate. This may be your legacy to your children. It's a great way to make up for lost time if you are near retirement and don't mind handling complaints of tenants.

The second way is to buy high-quality real estate before the market has recognized its quality and wait for the market to catch up. This is like buying stock in a company with lots of growth potential. It's Tier-Two-style investing. It requires recognizing future hot locations or other special features that will cause growth in value beyond normal inflation. Alternatively, it requires the purchase of a handyman special and an up-to-the-minute sprucing up. It also requires that you be able to hold the property while you are waiting for the world to discover its worth.

The Tier-Three way to make up for lost time in real estate is to buy distressed or otherwise undervalued properties and sell them immediately. In fact, you may even "flip" the contract: Sell your right to buy without even having closed on the real estate and taken ownership.

These three ways of making up for lost time in real estate require very different approaches to leverage and inflation.

To get you started, I have outlined three scenarios that you can duplicate to make up for lost time in each of the three tiers. Not all will be for everyone, and none may be appropriate for you. But if any are, you've got a gold mine in your future.

TIER-ONE INVESTING IN REAL ESTATE

You are about to enter the world of multiple dwellings. Select a stable blue-collar area within commuting distance from your own home. I like a well-kept multifamily white elephant in a town or near the center of a suburban village. If you live in a big city, where multiple dwellings are out of your price range, consider a well-maintained building in a minority ghetto. With a minority partner, you may even get government funding. If you yourself qualify, go for it.

Since you are seeking a relatively safe Tier-One investment, choose a building that already has a rent roll that supports its cost. Make sure that the property needs something: better management, construction, refurbishment. Anything that will help you raise rents as each tenant moves out.

Don't be afraid to hire a "ten-percenter." That is a person who will manage the property for 10 percent of the rent roll while you are away or retire to another location. As an alternative, if you are close to retirement, choose a multiple dwelling near your retirement haven and hire the ten-percenter right away. When you retire, you can take over the management.

Insider Tips for Tier-One Real Estate Investors

Ordinary foreclosures and distress sales are generally not your cup of tea. Instead, watch for estate sales. These are usually excellent properties that were liquidated under duress because the decedent's estate couldn't pay the death taxes. Watch your local law journals (found at courthouse newsstands and those located near courthouses) for ads. Then, don't make the same mistake that the deceased owner made. Stay liquid enough to pay the estate tax or to buy an insurance property so your family won't have to sell if they inherit the property.

Let estate attorneys know of your interest in such property. Your local bar association will give you a list of trust and estate lawyers. They are generally the attorneys who handle estate sales. Send each a professional letter offering to buy multiple dwellings at a fair price if his or her clients must liquidate. Make friends with local insurance brokers; they also know when one of their clients has a distressed property that may go into estate sale.

Learn to market your building. Sometimes an inexpensive building that is well-appointed and located in a convenient neighborhood attracts upscale rents even though the neighborhood itself is downscale. Or locate a prestige building in a stigmatized neighborhood and market it to the working affluent. Safety and security features together with style will work. Such an approach is called "gentrification." It has been successful everywhere from Hell's Kitchen in New York City to Pioneer Square in Seattle, Washington.

The key to Tier-One real estate investing is to buy well, manage well, and know how to collect rents, since you will probably never sell!

TIER-TWO INVESTING IN REAL ESTATE

Tier-Two investing is growth investing. That means that you must find something undervalued today that the world will appreciate tomorrow. In the eighties that could have been almost anything. Today things are different.

The old rule for quality real estate was simple: "location, location, location." In a funny moment in a *Cheers* episode, actor Woody Harrelson comments: "Don't the real estate people know those are all one thing?" If they didn't know it then, they know it now. Quality of management is also important today, although location still counts as number one. Here are other things people are looking for, whether they plan to rent or buy:

Environmental Considerations: The new buyer wants everything from energy efficiency to nature trails.

Ease of Maintenance: Expensive and difficult-to-maintain housing is a white elephant even in wealthy areas.

Family Values: Good schools, parks, good neighbors, and safety are primary in the "school-aged" family.

Innovative Communal Developments: Shared housing, in which several families live together and pool resources under a variety of circumstances, are the rage in parts of the far west. Co-housing, individual ownership in communities that provide shared resources like child care and elder care, are catching on. The original model is a Norwegian development. To learn more about investing in such New Age housing, read Kathryn McCamant and Charles Durrett, *Cohousing: A Contemporary Approach to Housing Ourselves* (Berkeley: Habitat Press, 1988). The real estate newsletter that networks New Age real estate seekers is *Networker*, CRSP, P.O. Box 27731, Los Angeles, CA 90027; 213-738-1254.

"Hoffices": The home office community is the mecca of the future. These are single homes or cooperative apartments that can share fax machines and telecommunications and even meet at the communal water cooler.

Second Homes for Retirement: Selecting a second home location early, and renting to the extent possible, makes a good substitute for an unaffordable first home. If you can own both, so much the better. As America ages and people do not make up for lost time, there will be numerous older renters ready to fill your retirement apartment or housing space.

Global Investing: The rest of the world is getting older, too, and many middle-aged Americans dream of retiring abroad. Apply the same quality criteria to international properties as you do to domestic ones and watch the income come in from rentals. Eventually, you may use the property for your retirement. But buy abroad where you enjoy the lifestyle— that's your main criterion.

TIER-THREE INVESTING IN REAL ESTATE

To make money fast in real estate, you need "almost" a miracle. You need to buy low and sell high immediately. There are many ways to buy low. They include buying from the IRS, buying real estate owned by banks (REO), and buying foreclosures from the owner or at auction. The Bibliography will lead you to lots of methods.

Foreclosure

To get started, here are the fundamentals of foreclosure buying. It's easy to find foreclosure property and buy from the owner before a forced sale. Newspapers advertise properties, in courthouses you will find notices of sheriff's sales and notices of equity or trust sales. The know-how factor is important. For a lazy but worthwhile way to find foreclosures, subscribe to services like Daily Default Infoservice, P.O. Box 456, Antioch, CA 94509; 415-754-7039. Once you have selected a property, learn all you can about it from information in the county assessor's office or use DAMAR, a computer service (213-380-7105 or 1-800-873-2627) for a profile of the property and comparable ones in the area. When you have a thorough understanding of what you plan to buy, including the liens on the property, negotiate with the owner.

Next, you must know how to sell high. The following are two very different ways to do this.

The Flip Factor

Find an undervalued piece of real estate using the FISBO, RTC, REO, or foreclosure method. Enter into a contract to buy. The idea is to sell your right to buy (flip the contract) before closing. Be sure you can afford to close in the event that no one intervenes to buy you out prior to closing. That means you will have to have a financing clause in the contract. Eventually, you will be known as a purveyor of undervalued properties and will have potential buyers using you as a scout to buy for them. At first, however, you will have to be able to close or be prepared to lose your deposit.

People who make big money this way can do it without ever owning a piece of property. They do, though, own the right to buy. Another, similar method of Tier-Three real estate investing is owning an option to buy. If it expires in the time you hold the option, you lose the option price. If you can sell your right to buy, you have made a good deal of money with very little risk. This is an excellent way to make money in real estate if you have poor credit but a knack for selecting properties. The mortgage will be taken by the actual buyer, based on his or her credit worthiness.

The Quick Turnaround Factor

For those with good credit and the financial ability to close, a less risky Three-Tier method with real estate is to actually close and own the property. However, this must be done with the know-how of reselling at an immediate profit. Either you must be a good decorator and increase the appeal of a dull property with low-cost "drop-dead decorating," or you must be a handyman who can make a silk purse out of a sow's ear. The third, and hardest, way is to be a great marketer and build a rent roll where there was none. In the past, if you were a tough guy, you could quickly increase the value of property by getting rid of low-paying tenants and increasing rents.

Do All Three. The fact is that the real winners in real estate dabble in all three tiers of investing and are also diversified in non–real estate investments. Let's hope that this is a beginning of a long and happy diversified relationship with real estate.

AND NOW FOR SOMETHING COMPLETELY DIFFERENT

Before I end this chapter, I made up a question for myself so that I could best express my view of how to make up for lost time in real estate. Here is the question and the answer.

Q: Adriane, you have made and lost so much money in real estate, yet you still believe in its ability to make up for lost time. If you had your choice, what is the one real estate investment you would make?

A: *I would use a little-known investment strategy called "selling life estates." It works this way.*

I would buy well-maintained condominium units in excellent retirement areas throughout the world. If I could get good deals, I would also buy single-family residences. I would look in places such as Texas, North Carolina, Georgia, Louisiana, the San Juan Islands off the coast of Seattle, Portugal, and Mexico.

I would not sell the property. I would make a profit by selling a "life estate" in the property. A life estate is the renter's right to live in the property all of his or her life. The purchase price of the life estate would consist of two figures: a down payment and a monthly charge. This charge would increase over the years like rent, but it would be capped. The payments would fluctuate according to an index, much like an adjustable rate mortgage.

My market would be the millions of people worldwide who would need to cash out and use the proceeds on their homes to invest for retirement income. These people are home owners at heart and want the security of a permanent dwelling. They also want to keep costs closed-ended while their income is fixed.

My plan would provide them with this security. They could live in a dwelling for life. When they died, the property would revert to me.

If they chose to move, they could sell the life estate for the number of years left according to an actuarial table based on their life expectancy. So, like a home owner, they would have equity to sell.

If all of this seems like work, it is. In the nineties, with real estate, there is no free lunch.

EPILOGUE

THE GLOBAL NEIGHBORHOOD:

INVESTING IN THE YEAR 2000

GLOBALIZATION—WHAT'S IN IT FOR YOU

If ever there was an investment strategy that appealed to our generation, it is global investing. Whether we started to travel on $5 dollars a day in college, or took the kids to Shakespeare country, we are comfortable abroad.

While our parents like to visit Alaska and Hawaii, give us a small town in the south of France. So, it will be easy for us to accept investments in stocks, banks, and real estate in other countries. We must, because diversification is one key to making up for lost time, and because the opportunities there are too good to pass up.

I predict that by the year 2000 or before we will routinely have foreign bank accounts, annuities, and stocks. Already, global mutual funds are offered by professionals as part of the standard recommendation for retirement savings. Corporate pension funds have substantial investments in domestic and foreign stocks and bonds.

Don't ignore 55 percent of the world's financial opportunities. In order to make up for lost time, you must not think of global investments as exotic or extraordinary. They must be part of your portfolio right now. It is possible to invest globally in all three tiers. Most Asians and Europeans do so on a regular basis.

For many of you, the investment opportunities in Tier-Three stocks of other nations is not the only reason to go global. As you research your retirement living arrangements, you may find that cost and quality of life lead you to consider retirement abroad. Your safe Tier Ones are subject to buying power erosion if foreign currencies strengthen against the dollar.

Many of you are ready to invest globally; the only thing stopping you is convenience. Some years ago I became a speaker and writer for the Oxford Club. It is an exclusive club for international investors. Since then I have traveled to many foreign venues to explore opportunities. If you are interested in sophisticated foreign travel, let me know with a letter sent to the address on page 272.

Through the club, I learned easy ways for you to invest globally in the Three-Tier method without ever leaving your living room.

TIER-ONE GLOBAL INVESTING

Foreign banks offer accounts, money markets, and certificates of deposit just as our banks do. You open an account with U.S. currency and it buys the equivalent in foreign currency. The deposit will earn interest as it would at home, often a great deal more. Not every bank in every country is recommended. Government stability is crucial. That is why the favored choices for true diversification are England, Switzerland, Canada, the Netherlands, Germany, France, and Japan or Korea.

Once in a while, a country offers a huge interest rate compared to all others. Mexico did that in 1990. However, there is always a danger that as with Mexico, the deposit will be redeemed in undervalued currency (pesos) and buy back fewer dollars than were deposited. My rule is to go for the stable currency with the moderate interest rate.

Also, without FDIC insurance, a foreign bank must be chosen for its balance sheet. Since the S&L crisis, many of us are questioning the soundness of our own institutions. We should question foreign ones even more. Get the financial statement of any bank you select. You may request it directly from the bank. Don't be afraid to do so. U.S. banks often have less reserve and are in worse shape than foreign banks precisely because our FDIC system brings them consumer credibility and so they take more risks. Foreign banks must earn a reputation among their citizens. Some have been in business since the Middle Ages. Many are also privately insured. You'll learn all of this from the financial statement.

In 1990, U.S. banks were authorized to open accounts in foreign currency. Furthermore, a foreign currency account in a U.S. bank is FDIC-insured. One pioneer bank in the market is the Mark Twain Bank, 1630 South Lindbergh Boulevard, St. Louis, MO 63131. It offers twenty currencies and requires $10,000 minimum deposits.

If you are comfortable with Canadian banks, they all offer deposits, money markets, and certificates of deposits in the major European currencies.

If you want to put a toe in the water, consider the Royal Trust Bank of Austria, which has a minimum deposit of $3,000 and twelve currency choices. Write to Royal Trust Bank, P.O. Box 306 A-1011, Vienna, Austria, or call 43-143-6161. To purchase foreign currency or open a foreign bank account, write Michael Checkan, International Financial Consultants, 1700 Rockville Pike, Suite 400, Rockville, MD 20852, and ask for the free newsletter.

All transactions can be completed by fax, phone, or mail. For those looking for even greater diversity, invest in a foreign currency mutual fund. They are bought in the United States, and all the usual rules apply.

MAKE SURE YOUR FOREIGN INVESTMENT IS REALLY A TIER ONE

Back to basics: Tier Ones are predictable, stuffy, and goal-oriented investments. That means that when you diversify into foreign investing, you must do so with little risk of currency fluctuation. Naturally, foreign investing can be volatile because the value of the currency changes relative to the value of U.S. currency. Here's how it works:

You invest $10,000 in an English bank at 7 percent. The bank converts your dollars into pounds. When the investment matures or when you withdraw from an account, you then reconvert the pounds to dollars. This can result in a gain or loss in principal if the value of the pound to the dollar is different from what it was on the date you made your deposit. To hedge against currency volatility, you can keep your Tier-One foreign investing in a short-term global income fund. These keep the dollar-based value as steady as possible by diversifying and buying currency options.

There are mutual funds bought in the usual way. You can also buy foreign bonds, including zero-coupon bonds, and foreign bond mutual funds. However, you will always be playing the currency market with these.

I still like them as a diversification of your Tier-One portfolio, provided that you have established a large position in U.S. bonds and want to sprinkle the Tier-One assets with a little seasoning.

At present, it is illegal to sell fixed-income foreign annuities in the United States. That may change. A representative Swiss annuity that I follow has averaged 6 percent in total return tax-deferred for many years. The guaranteed interest rate was only 4 percent but our shrinking dollar added a yearly 2 percent gain as the Swiss franc strengthened.

TIER-TWO GLOBAL INVESTING

Tier-Two global investing means investing in stocks of foreign companies. At the moment, the most popular and simple way to do this is by using the mutual fund. The information regarding domestic mutual funds applies to foreign mutual funds as well. One note to remember: A "global" fund may invest in both foreign and U.S. companies. If you want solely foreign companies, look for an "international" fund. Better yet, read the prospectus to learn the holdings.

Individual country funds are also available. These offer more risk, more reward, less diversification. If you believe in the growth of a particular country, or of a particular industry in a particular country (at the time of this writing, the building and cement industry in Mexico is very inviting), you can invest in a "unit trust." These are not SEC-regulated and cannot sell to you directly. Your foreign bank, however, can purchase these shares with the money in your account.

If you are interested in individual shares of stock, you can buy from a foreign stock exchange. Most brokers can place an order for you. In addition, you can buy American depository receipts (ADRs). These are receipts that show ownership in the stock of a foreign corporation. They are issued in dollars by U.S. banks and physically kept in the bank's foreign depository. They are U.S. securities and have all the protections of the Securities Investor Protection Corporation (SIPC).

To buy ADRs, you place an order with your regular broker, who in turn places an order with a foreign broker. Many ADRs are listed on the stock exchanges, although the underlying shares of the foreign corporations are not.

Once they are purchased, the bank deposits the actual shares in an off-shore branch and holds them for you. The ADR is your receipt.

The procedure is simple for you: The ADR is registered in your name instead of in the riskier bearer form in which most foreign stocks are registered. You can sell with a phone call. Moreover, you get immediate price quotes and dividends paid in dollars.

Be aware that not all ADRs are created equal. Some are listed on a stock exchange. If they are, the company's financials must be disclosed according to generally accepted U.S. accounting principles. You can follow listed ADRs in the regular daily financial journals. Others are also sponsored by the foreign corporation whose shares they represent. If so, you will receive reports in English.

Unlisted and unsponsored ADRs result from the company's unwillingness to meet U.S. reporting and disclosure standards. Some of the best companies don't bother—Nissan, Toyota, and Nestlé, for example.

In sum, there are unlisted/unsponsored ADRs that you will learn about through reading and via your broker's advice, and listed/sponsored ADRs found in the financial dailies. A few unsponsored but listed ADRs exist. Those companies need not (but often do) send you reports as they would their foreign investors. Their reporting standards are their own.

Warning: One ADR does not necessarily equal one share of stock. Do not compare the price of one ADR in one company to the price of one ADR in another company. Find out how many shares are bought by an ADR, then divide the price by that number. Also, stock warrants and stock rights that may come with a stock represented by an ADR cannot be exercised by the U.S. shareholder. The issuer splits off the right and sells it separately.

TIER-THREE GLOBAL INVESTING

Here's where things get interesting. You can speculate in foreign currency and even in foreign currency futures. This is done by purchasing futures contracts from your broker or "forward exchange contracts" from a bank.

In buying futures you can purchase any actively traded currency on the International Money Market Division of the Chicago Mercantile Exchange. The contracts are delivered on the third Wednesday of every fourth month. You need to put only 3 percent of the purchase price down. The current exchange rate sets the price. If the currency has risen in value relative to the dollar, you can sell the contract or take delivery and hold the currency. You win. If the currency has decreased in value, sell the contract at a loss and take a hit for the difference between the contract price and sale price.

The currency futures market is the fastest and wildest Tier Three I've ever found. Government elections, inflation within the country, treaties, and the price of oil are just a few examples of what drives currency rates. But the real excitement comes in cross trading futures contracts in different currencies.

For even more action with less money invested, use the same option system we learned in speed investing. Buy an option on a futures contract in a foreign currency if you believe that the value will rise in relationship to the dollar. Buy puts if you think the currency is weak in relationship to the dollar.

Words of wisdom: I cannot imagine anyone who is serious about making up for lost time not including some form of foreign investing in his or her plan. The fact is that at least 55 percent of all investing opportunities are abroad. If you ignore this, you are operating with one hand tied behind your back. In my opinion, investing abroad is not unpatriotic. You are actually investing in the United States's most important commodity: you, its citizen.

BIBLIOGRAPHY

CAREER

Angle, Susan, and Alex Hiram. *Adventure Careers*. Hawthorne, NJ: Career Press, 1992.

Bolles, Richard. *What Color Is Your Parachute?* Berkeley: Ten Speed Press, 1989.

Gordon, Harley. *How to Protect Your Life Savings from Catastrophic Illness and Nursing Homes*. Boston: Financial Planning Institute, Inc., 1990.

Satterfield, Mark. *Where the Jobs Are*. Hawthorne, NJ: Career Press, 1992.

Shambhala, Doil. *The Lotus and the Pool*. Washington, DC: Palindrome Press, 1992.

Sinetar, Marsha. *Do What You Love, The Money Will Follow*. New York: Dell, 1987.

BUDGETING

Hunt, Mary. *The Best of the Cheap-Skate Monthly*. New York: St. Martin's Press, 1993.

Lazar, Elysa, and Eve Miceli. *Outlet Shoppers Guide*. New York: Lazar Media Group, 1992.
————. *Shop by Mail*. New York: Lazar Media Group, 1992.

BANKRUPTCY

Ventura, John. *Fresh Start*. Chicago: Dearborn Financial Publishers, 1992.

ECONOMIC INDICATORS

Michaels, Donald. *Investing in Uncertain Times*. Chicago: Longman Financial Services Publishing, 1988.

FOR YOUR PARENTS

Berg, Adriane G. *Warning: Dying May Be Hazardous to Your Wealth*. Hawthorne, NJ: Career Press, 1992.
Blum, Laurie. *Free Money for Diseases of Aging*. New York: Simon & Schuster, 1992.
Boue, Alexander A. *The Medicaid Planning Handbook*. Boston: Little, Brown & Company, 1992.
Gordon, Harley. *How to Protect Your Life Savings from Catastrophic Illness and Nursing Homes*. Boston: Financial Planning Institute Inc., 1990.
Levy, Michael, M.D. *Parenting Mom and Dad*. New York: Prentice Hall Press, 1991.
Skala, Ken. *American Guidance for Seniors*. Falls Church, VA: American Guidance, Inc., 1991.
Stock, Barbara. *It's Easy to Avoid Probate*. Winter Park, FL: Linch Publishing, Inc., 1985.

MONEY FOR EDUCATION

Blum, Laurie. *Free Money for College*. New York: Facts on File, 1990.
Cassidy, Daniel J. *The Scholarship Book*. 3d ed. Englewood Cliffs, NJ: Prentice Hall, 1990.
McKee, Cynthia Ruiz, and Phillip C. McKee, Jr. *Cash for College*. New York: Hearst Books, 1993.

HOW TO USE REAL ESTATE IN YOUR IRA

Scavazzo, John. *The Real Estate IRA*. New York: Dodd, Mead and Company, 1987.

MORE INSIGHT INTO OUR CULTURE

Lapman, Lewis. *Money and Class in America*. New York: Weidenfeld & Nicolson, 1988.
Newman, Katherine. *Falling from Grace*. New York: Free Press, 1988.

MONEY AND PSYCHOLOGY

Lieberman, Annette, and Vicki Linder. *Unbalanced Accounts*. New York: Penguin Books, 1987.

MONEY AND THE SPIRIT

Phillips, Michele. *The Seven Laws of Money*. New York: Random House, 1974.

Q AND A FROM A GURU

Altfest, Lewis, and Karen Altfest. *Lew Altfest Answers All Your Questions About Money*. New York: McGraw-Hill, 1987.

REAL ESTATE INVESTMENTS

Bloch, Sonny, and Carolyn Janik. *How You Can Profit from the S&L Bailout*. New York: Bantam Books, 1991.
Irwin, Robert. *Buy, Rent & Hold*. New York: McGraw-Hill, 1991.
Thomas, Ted. *Foreclosure Gold Mining*. Danville, CA: New Growth Financial, 1992.

RELOCATION

Rosenberg, Lee, and Sara Lee Rosenberg. *Destination Florida*. Clearwater, FL: Rex Publishing Company, 1989.
———. *50 Fabulous Places to Raise Your Family*. Hawthorne, NJ: Career Press, 1993.

BLOCKBUSTERS—A LITTLE OF EVERYTHING

Berg, Adriane G. *Your Wealth-Building Years*. New York: Newmarket Press, 1990.
———. *Financial Planning for Couples*. New York: Newmarket Press, 1993.

Philips, Carole. *The New Money Workbook for Women*. Andover, MA: Brick House Publishing Company, 1988.

Quinn, Jane Bryant. *Making the Most of Your Money*. New York: Simon & Schuster, 1991.

Savage, Terry. *Terry Savage's New Money Strategies for the 90's*. New York: Harper Business, 1991.

BUDGET

Bankers Secret Newsletter, P.O. Box 78, Elizaville, NY 12523.

Levy, Frank. *Dollars and Dreams: The Changing American Income Distribution*. New York: W.W. Norton & Company, 1988.

Nicholas, Donald. *Investing in Uncertain Times*. New York: Longman Financial Services, 1988.

ESTATE PLANNING

Berg, Adriane G. *The Complete Parents' and Grandparents' Guide to Investing for Children*. (Audiotape series; for information, call 1-800-934-2211.)

———. *Saving the Family Fortune*. (Audiotape series; for information, call 1-800-934-2211).

INDEX

All of the ideas in this book share one golden thread: the presentation of tools for making up for lost time. If you know some unique methods, suggestions, or inspiring stories to help make up for lost time, please let me know. I would like to include you in my circle of MUFLT friends, whom I met in places as diverse as communes and boardrooms while researching this book.

If you have a question, to the extent I can, I will answer it. New information that you bring to my attention will surely be incorporated into future newsletters, books, or broadcast material. In this way, we can form a network of people who have made up for lost time. As you see from the stories in this book, it can be done, it has been done, and you will do it. But you will need all the help you can get. So take it, because it is offered with sincerity and friendship.

If you want to be in touch, please write:

Adriane G. Berg
Suite 533
358 Seventh Avenue
New York, N.Y. 10003